Precious Poetic Moments

Briefly Suspended

in an Abstract Called Time

Thomas Paul Monday

Copyright 2014 by Thomas Paul Monday

All rights reserved. This book or parts thereof may not be reproduced in any form, stored in a retrieval system, or transmitted in any form by any means-electronic, mechanical, photographic, photocopy, recording, or otherwise-without prior written permission of the author. If you would like to use material from the book (other than for review purposes), prior written permission must be obtained by contacting the publisher at books@knowledgepowerbooks.com.

Thank you for your support of the author's rights.

Published by Knowledge Power Books
A Division of Knowledge Power Communications, Inc.
25379 Wayne Mills Place, Suite 131
Valencia, CA 91355
www.knowledgepowerbooks.com

ISBN: 978-0-9907199-2-2
Library of Congress Control Number:
Edited by: Penny Scott
Cover and Interior Design: John Sibley, Rock Solid Productions

Printed in the United States of America

Table of Contents

Dedication	
Acknowledgements	
In Christ Always	1
A Teacher Named, Larry	3
Byron and Georgia	4
Wolfgang	5
Blessed	6
James and Dani – True to the Commitment of Love	7
Amara	8
The Gift	9
An Angel Called Blessed – Celebrating the Life of Joann	10
Fond Memories in the Stillness of the Night	12
You've Been Faithful and True	13
Mama, What do Angels Do?	14
A Beautiful Star Called Esther	15
Erma	16
The Victory XII	17
The Day MaKenzie Came from Heaven	19
Natural and Free	20
Reflection for the Soul	21
January 22, 2004	22
January 16, 2004	23
I'll Rest in Him, Until the Morning, Mabel	24
George and Gracie	26
Chunte	28
The Portrait of an Angel	29
Coretess, A Precious Gem	30
Sherry	31
Lamar	32
Milton	34

Kevin	35
Brian	36
Mechael, Your Daddy's Little Girl	37
Wishing You the Very Best	38
Daddy's Little Girl	39
Aliya	40
Congratulation, Mrs. Coffee	41
Phil, Ask Me if I Care	42
Genevieve	43
Noah	44
Yvette – Angelic Beauty in Any Language	45
George	46
In Memory of a Wonderful and Loving Son-in-Law	47
Barbara	48
Eva	50
A Reflection in Time – In Loving Memory of Erma	51
That Early Morning Flight – In Loving Memory of Carmen	52
The Legacy of This Man – In Loving Memory of Mr. Robert	53
In the Mirror of the Heart – Dedicated to Jardine Charles	54
Sugar Doesn't Come Any Sweeter	55
Hannah	56
Mama Clara	57
Take A Chance With Me	58
Precious – Priceless Little Survivor	59
It's Official	60
God Sent a Very Precious Little Girl - Layla	61
Allen David	62
My Loving Dad, Eldrew	63
Audrey, Here We Go Again	64
Happy Birthday, Chemina	65
Nelda, A Living Portrait of Beauty Revealed	66

A Reflective Fragrance - Billie	67
The Coach	68
A Celebration of Life, James – I'll Keep the Faith Until We Meet Again	70
The Lighthouse of My Soul - Jack	71
The Sun Will Continue to Shine, After Every Rough Stormy Rainy Day – Charlotte and Lucky	72
Elaine: A Priceless Gift of Enduring Love	74
Abstract of a Thankful Heart	76
A Smile Made of Pure Gold	77
I Want to Be Just Like You, Horn	79
If the Heavenly Father Truly Didn't Care, Patricia	81
Eternal Loving – Memory of Coach	83
Thank You Daryl for the Beautiful Landscape Design of my Home: It's A Job Well Done	84
A Final Thought	86
Glory Land Bound	88
Got Time for a Dime	90
Regrets	91
Honey in High Heels	92
Special Person	93
The Radiance of Beauty	94
Alone	95
Diamonds, Roses and a Cube of Sugar – From the Entire Challenger School Staff	96
If it Were Possible, the Two of Us	97
Oh Bless the Lord My Debt Was Paid in Full – Praise His Holy Name - Ricky	98
Change Might Be A Necessity, but Here's My Final Thought	100
The Eternal Twins they Call Henry and Ed	101
A Quiet Soft Spoken Gentile Giant	103
A Precious Gift, He Gave to Me	105

A Source of Unconditional Enduring Love	107
A Temporary Loan from Heaven, Edna	109
Something that Mama Once Said	111
Tears	112
That Fall from Grace	113
Tricia If It Were Possible, the Two of Us, In Memory of Eldrew	114
A Co-Worker, Neighbor, Mentor and Friend	115
The Day Mother Became An Angel	116
Though I Walk Through the Valley of the Giants	118
A Smile for Jessie	120
Pure Beauty in Flight	121
A Rose for All Times	122
Evelyn – All Is Well – My Big Sister	123
About The Author	125

Dedication

I would like to dedicate this book to the precious memory of my mother. She was a tremendous source of encouragement and inspiration toward my academic growth. It was my mother, who first introduced me to the love, mercy and lasting grace of a creative and eternal God. "The Great I Am," who before the very foundations of the World were even formed created a redemptive plan to save the lost.

Thanks Mama!

Love Always,

TPM

Acknowledgements

Over the past 60-plus years of living on planet Earth, my life has been profoundly enriched through the acquaintances, lives, and wisdom, of a countless number individuals. Many are still alive, and some are now deceased. Your infinite words of encouragement, wisdom, advice and numerous acts of loving kindness, will always be appreciated and remembered. I consider each one of you very precious and unique. Each one of you will always hold a special place of remembrance in the sacred treasure chest of the heart.

I'm truly eternally grateful.

A Very Special Thanks

I would like to give a special, "thank you," to the entire staff at Knowledge Power Books, Inc., for affording me the opportunity, and the assistance to help complete a dream that I've had for years, to finally become a reality. I would also like to thank my various family members, friends, and co-workers, who over the years have been continuous sources of inspiration, encouragement and a fountain of positive constructive feedback. There is no amount of words to write, that could remotely come close to describing my gratitude of just how much each of you have contributed to the enrichment of my life.

Thank you!

To each and every one of you,

Love always

TPM

Precious Poetic Moments

In Christ Always, Clarence

The very day that we were born, the Harbor Master set the human ship loose (free), to sail the earthly seas of life, with its final destination – eternity.

These old, fragile ships of dirt and clay, set sail, laden with cargo: some mental, some physical, or both, is tossed to and fro, by the various trials and tribulations we encounter, while on the turbulent sea called life.

As captain of the ship, it's His responsibility to ensure that all the hatches are battened down; the anchor is pulled up; and the main sail has been lowered into position. All these precautions are necessary in order to ensure that the crew and cargo eventually arrive safely at its designated port of call, or harbor of rest.

A good captain has read and carefully studied his maps and charts (His Bible, the Word), when planning the route, noting in detail the various dangers that can be expected along the way.

We, as crew members, play an important role, while aboard this earthly ship. However, once the crew has signed on, it's the captain that who assumes all responsibility for carrying the load, and who deals with the thoughts of pain, suffering, worry, lack and even death itself.

Perhaps, that's why He is identified by so many different names; Lord, King of Kings, The Good Master, The Good Shepherd, Jesus, Savior, Lord of Lords, The Alpha and The Omega, The Holy One of Israel, The Bright and Shining Morning Star, and The Hope of Glory, just to name a few. Loved one, don't cry or weep for me. I'm in good hands, I had decided a long, long time ago, that Jesus Christ would be the captain of my ship and Lord of my life.

Thomas Paul Monday

Christ and Christ alone is the only one, who can carry all of my burdens: calm all of life's storms, while at the same time, bringing me home safely, to that harbor garden paradise of eternal peace and rest.

In Christ, Always.

A Teacher Named, Larry

There are very few people of integrity, who are blessed in this short span of time that we call life: to be entrusted with the keys of opportunity, and who possess the truly rare gifts to teach and share.

Very rarely in the ranks of the truly professional educator are there satisfaction in just imparting knowledge alone, without demonstrating the beauty and love for life.

The affection and care for what and how information is delivered to one's students, can be reflected through the patient eyes of love for an occupation, which by its very nature, must be able to affect change. And at the same time, touch the lives of all, with words of encouragement and hope.

Neither silver nor gold can compare, with the warmth that is derived from a simple smile of understanding and words of encouragement. Not enough words accurately vocalize the appreciation friends, co-workers or students get from unselfishly sharing, the many years of skilled experience as a professional musician, educator, and artist.

It is therefore, a privilege and an honor for me, to call a teacher named Larry, a fellow co-worker and a friend.

Thomas Paul Monday

Byron and Georgia

While listening to the soft, soothing sounds of music, my thoughts reflect back to the goodness and mercy of God. These thoughts concerning the mercy and goodness of the true nature of our Heavenly Father opened the floodgates of emotions. Soon, emotions were overflowing into the storehouse of my very soul.

I was overwhelmed with gratitude regarding God's blessings of health. I'm thankful for God's immeasurable depth of love: which allows Him to send His only Son to Earth to die such a cruel death on the cross to justify and redeem the lost. The mere thought of God's mercy and His goodness, concerning the promises found in His Word, as taught by the Comforter, through the Fruits of The Holy Spirit, compel me to just want to give Him continuous praise.

When I think of God's mercy, His goodness and how He blesses me in so many ways, I realize just how much He has blessed Barbara and me when He introduced us to the two of the sweetest individuals, this side of heaven.

Byron, thanks to Georgia and you, Barbara and I have been able to better appreciate what our Heavenly Father has planned for us to enjoy in Glory, and for all of eternity. Byron and Georgia, our thoughts on mercy and goodness of our Heavenly Father rush from our lips, and quickly rise upwards into the sky, in the form of praise: like incense escaping from the altar of a sacred fire, while worshipping the Creator of all things.

May you continue to minister to all that you meet, through your God-given talents and gifts, and may you continue to be a blessing to others, through the Holy Spirit, and the Fruits of His Spirit.

Wolfgang

Sitting in my recliner; anxious, excitedly waiting, anticipating with awe and wonder, sensing each passing moment of time that reverberates from the second hand, as it makes its way around the face of the clock.

Tic-Toc-Tic-Toc: how much longer, can I, just I, be forced to wait before I receive that special call? My thoughts of my, little girl now an adult, married, and soon, a proud mother with a son of her very own.

Tic-Toc-Tic-Toc: my thoughts of joy, laughter and countless memories are all eternal, with each one covering a brief moment in that reality we so fondly refer to as "time."

These thoughts, which engulf yesterday, today and even tomorrow, rise silently like smoke: from a smoldering fire, into the stillness of the night air, and slowly disappear.

Realizing that you live just one or two states away, offers me a little comfort, and yet in my soul, it still feels like some strange, foreign and distant land. Like any proud parent. I get really excited and happy, when I hear that Michael, and you are doing well. Always stay in love and together, support one another as a family. In unity, you'll be able to take on and defeat each and every adversity.

At 2:10 a.m., January 7, 2004, I finally received that special call, notifying me, "Not to worry," that it's official: I'm a new Grand Pa. Sherry just gave birth to a fine, healthy baby boy and his name is Wolfgang.

Thomas Paul Monday

Blessed

There is something truly wonderful about being blessed. You're safe and secure in the light of His love: even when surrounded by countless foes, silently lurking and hiding during periods of vulnerability that wreak havoc, and doubt, primarily, during the dark stillness of the night. A quiet still voice, tells you not to fret or worry, and reminds you that you're still a King's daughter and, therefore, everything is going to be all right.

The last night of the year just before midnight: of the year, 2006 was given a last bow: a final symbolic curtain call. And was granted permission to slip quietly from the spotlight of this world's center stage, into that other dimension called eternity.

I watched the second hand on the clock, move the hour hand closer and closer to another New Year. I began to reflect on people, places and significant events that in one way or another had a profound impact on my life over this past year.

My thoughts start to bubble upwards toward the surface of my spirit; thoughts far, far too plenty to even account. My thoughts continue to flow as if divinely timed and released from some deep artesian well: predestined and majestically hidden, somewhere within the treasure chest of the soul.

It was as if His voice spoke to me, saying, "Gabby is blessed because she has been a blessing to so many others. She's blessed going out and coming in. She's blessed, she's blessed!"

James and Dani, True to the Commitment of Love

Real Love, I'm told has the supernatural ability to simultaneously bridge that mystical, abstract called reality, not being bound by the natural laws of time, distance and space.

Actual commitments of real love like pure refined gold, is precious and very, very, rare. My thoughts concerning the matter of real love, after much discussion and considerable meditation, are too numerous even to be contained on this simple sheet of paper. You have the gifts of joy and laughter.

Precious loving memories, and countless thoughts, continue to reside unhindered within the treasure chest of the heart, like the youthful movements of innocence children involved in endless hours of play, which ultimately results in healing to the body and the soul.

James and Dani: the two of you are loved by all who know you. You have the respect of a loving family, co-workers and countless friends. We stand together, united as one, generating prayers and support for such a beautiful couple, still so wildly in love. Precious thoughts of love are always collectively, eternally bound together for strength, to demonstrate love and support.

Our prayers and thoughts, like smoke escaping from a sacred fire, burning on the eternal altar of soul: rise slowly, uninterruptedly, into the safety of the heavens, as lasting testimonials that real love, make a commitment forever and ever.

Thomas Paul Monday

Amara

While holding my newborn granddaughter for the very first time, thoughts of joy and ecstasy, too numerous to even be contained on this single sheet of paper began to rise like smoke, from the eternal flame of my soul, into the stillness of the night sky. In times of great sadness, or trials, God will often send his angels to deliver joy to humanity, unannounced, and in the purest of forms.

Only the Lord knows when the time is perfect and just right to heal a wounded or broken heart. How can one accurately calculate, the eventual effect on humanity, that total innocence in the form of a new born child, will eventually have in this world.

I'm continually reflecting with love and joy, the everlasting memories of my newly-born granddaughter resting, lying peacefully on a grandpa's chest, listening patiently to the sweet rhythm of pride and great delight, continually erupting like fireworks, openly within the valley of my heart.

I'm so thankful to God that He sent one of His angels to earth, to give us just a little more joy, and I'm so proud that her name was called "Amara Grace."

The Gift

There are certain people who have been divinely given natural gifts and talents. Over the years, such individuals have been assigned various names by humanity, agents of mercy, helpers, messengers, and even angels, just to name a few. These divine gifts or talents were predestined before that concept call time was even conceived. And, may often vary significantly from one individual to another.

Please allow me a few moments, just to name a few of these natural, God-given gifts and talents. The warmth and comfort that naturally comes from the elegance of a smile; the soothing, friendly effect resulting from the beauty of the eyes, whose regenerating energy source, radiates continually from that eternal fountain, a quiet, scared place found only within the treasure chest of the soul; and the ability to be courteous and considerate.

The ability to listen, and respond with empathy and compassion: these highly-gifted and talented individuals are predestined to share these priceless treasures with everyone that they meet, in ways that very few can imagine. I recently met such an individual: a young lady by the name of Linda, who within a very short period of time, thoroughly convinced me, leaving no doubt in my mind, that she, too, was a divine holder and keeper of "the gift."

Thomas Paul Monday

An Angel Called Blessed, *Celebrating the Life of JoAnn*

I received the news the other day, concerning the homegoing of one of God's saints, Mrs. JoAnn. Reflecting on the news, I began to think what affect this precious lady's life had on so many others. My thoughts were far, far too numerous, and started to rise up within the eternal skies of my spirit: like steam, swiftly escaping from some crevice within the earth, only to then, silently disappear.

It was during this quiet stillness in the night, that a soothing sweet voice gently whispered into my spiritual ear, through the open door, leading to the treasure chest of the soul, "Don't fret or worry about me."

"Boy! Oh, boy! Oh, boy!"

Don't you know, that I'm a King's Daughter, with special privileges, that was setup from the beginning of time, therefore, with unwavering faith and confidence, I can tell you that everything has already been taken care of and I'm now in very good hands?

Boy! Oh, boy! Oh, boy!

"I'm absent from this physical body, but I'm resting with the eternal presence of the King of Kings, and the Lords of Lords."

Boy! Oh, boy! Oh, boy!

There is something truly wonderful and glorious concerning the life and legacy of Mrs. JoAnn. Mrs. JoAnn was divinely-blessed and in-turn, was truly a blessing to others. Mrs. JoAnn proudly bore the titles of a wife, mother, grandmother, nurse, giver, provider, Christian and a true, lifelong friend.

Mrs. JoAnn worked for years as a Registered Nurse (a true earthly Angel of Mercy), who took special pride in her professional appearance; continued professional growth and in providing excellence in professional nursing care to her patients.

Mrs. JoAnn was blessed and was truly a blessing to others.

Thomas Paul Monday

Fond Memories
In the Stillness of the Night

I set back within the comforts of my recliner. My thoughts rise like sacred smoke, into the still night sky, seeking escape from a raging fire somewhere on the altar of my soul. My thoughts attempt to make some kind of rational sense to the sudden, tragic death of a former co-worker and very close friend. Any feeble attempt on my part to use such a crude method, as with paper and pen, to capture the very essence of such a great humanitarian, is certainly doomed to failure, and could, therefore, only be classified as merely an attempt.

Countless thoughts and pictures, far too great to calculate, continually play within my mind: depicting a very kind and giving person. Charles P. and his loving wife, both gave generously of their time. Memories are vivid of his academic knowledge, his wood-working skills, his landscape knowledge, her professional talents as an accomplished artist and his political expertise to anyone who asked for help or advice.

I fondly recall attending numerous community fish fries, barbeques, and Fourth of July celebrations at the home of Charlie and his wife Nelda. Charlie and Nelda freely gave, so everyone that they meet feel loved.

Both Charlie and Nelda P. will continue to live forever within the confines of the heart, as sacred, fond, memories of countless neighbors, co-workers and friends, who also truly loved them!

You've Been Faithful and True

On this very special day of celebration, my reflections are too numerous to simply be contained on this one single sheet of paper. My thoughts, like smoke being forcibly expelled from flames engulfed logs on a cozy campfire, rise quickly into the stillness of the night sky.

How does one find the right words to accurately describe those natural God-given talents that are stored in the treasure chest of the soul, which ultimately affect and enrich the lives of so many? Truly you are a professional in every sense of the word: a living witness of us, what grace, compassion, determination, character, and hope can produce.

You are a mother, helper, educator, adviser, colleague, giver and a witness to humanity. If I could conjugate a basic sentence to describe and reflect the collective thoughts of how we feel about you as a part of the Challenger family, it would probably sound like this: "Diane, well done. You've weathered the storms of life for another year. You've stayed the course with patience and you've been faithful and true."

Personally, it is an honor and a privilege to call you a co-worker and a friend. Happy Birthday Diane!

Thomas Paul Monday

Mama, What Do Angels Do?

What route do angels take as they travel back-and-forth through the gates of Heaven carrying messages of hope, faith, and the answers to countless prayers? Angels are God's messengers, assigned the divine mission of assisting His people in dispersing the darkness in this world: through the power of His Word, and the elegance of His eternal light.

Angels are innumerable and fearless. They possess great strength and power. They are spirits and, therefore will never grow old or die. Oh yes, they can even travel great distances in the blink of an eye.

The Bible says that when one of the saints of the Most High dies, His angels then transports that weary soul to a place of peace, beauty and everlasting rest, while observing the majesty and elegance of a recent sunset. My thought began to travel back in time to my childhood. I began to grin childishly as I remembered so vividly numerous events, words of wisdom, and life lessons, that you had taught us in one way or another.

I'm glad you told us about God's love and what His Son did for all of mankind on the cross at Calvary. Mama, the length of time from your sunrise to your sunset has spanned over 95 years. What do angels do? I'm forever grateful you taught us, that when you are absent from the body, angels immediately transport you into the presence of the Lord.

A Beautiful Star Called, Esther

It has been said that a woman's name is a reflection of a small portion of the many beautiful gifts that are stored deep within the treasure chest of the soul. If in fact, this is the case, then some treasure chests must be overflowing with an abundance of these precious gifts, when compared to others. The other day while studying, I just happened to pick up an extremely powerful book, on a very wonderful and beautiful woman named Esther. This Esther is a Persian name and means "Star." The richness of this woman's, dedication to her god and family only added to the glory that she already possessed. I became deeply intrigued with the life of this woman, her contributions and the numerous talents that she possessed.

She was as a woman and mother, a strong role model for all of her children, and never once wavered in her love and devotion towards any of them. She was faithful with a little, and later was greatly blessed with much. She possessed and knew how to daily utilize the wisdom of God, towards the benefits of all her people. She recognized the true source of her strength, and had wisdom enough, to give her God the Glory, the thanks and the credit. People sought her advice and were blessed after her counsel. During the quiet, late hours of the night, my attentions are often drawn of the heavens. I'll notice one particularly bright star, which seems to stands out from all the others.

It's at this point, that I think of and feel the strongest, love, and respect of this beautiful woman called Esther, resting continually in the peace, wisdom and loving arms of her God. Then finally, I remember one kind of debt that I'd never be free of, the biggest debt of all, the one that I still owe, and the one that Jesus Christ paid in full when He died just for me.

Erma

Today is a very special day, for so many reasons. I have countless thoughts, emotions, and memories that take me back in time to the days, when we were growing up as children. While reclined and resting in my easy chair, I began to smile with a slight nod of the head. I started to reflect back in time. And yes, even from then until now, through the thick and thin, you have always been there for us. My memories are more valuable than any kind of precious metal or priceless stone.

The significance of this special day, celebrates the love that a big sister gave us, which resembled the love that only a natural mother could give. Thoughts of laughter, happiness and joy, surrounding the true significance of this day, rise into the sky like smoke from a smoldering fire, contained somewhere deep within the treasure chest of my soul. My thoughts and memories, unlike physical smoke that is visible for only a brief moment and then vanishes, will remain forever.

This day signifies the creative beginning a love and a dedication that has helped to shape all of us into who we are today. Excitedly, anticipating and preparing for this day, I've opened the door to the store house of my soul: in order to share with the whole world, just a few of the precious memories, and thoughts that are eternally stored.

We are extremely fortunate and blessed to have such a wonderful and caring sister like you in our lives.

Erma, Happy Birthday and May God bless you always.

The Victory XII

All eyes and thoughts were permanently fixed on the door in anticipation. Entering through the door with confidence and authority a new CEO; a strong, beautiful Black woman, commanding, dedicated and determined. Standing behind a brown, high-back chair, facing a long oak conference table, all of the room occupants were invited to sit down. They were all of one mind, earnest and totally consumed in their quest for truth.

The eloquent, but piercing words of enlightenment set ablaze and completely engulfed their hearts and spirits, forever, destroying, many rumors and outright lies. "Rania," a derivation of the Old English word "Rowena," which means "will know, friend," Stop, take note, for the hour has come. Notice is now being served to all. Whispers and nods of approval, spread throughout the crowd, like waves on a small pond, responding to the sudden impact of a stone. The room occupants stood with respect, as they looked at one another, in total amazement and disbelief.

An electrical charge of energy, containing self-confidence and boldness filled the atmosphere. It slowly invaded each individual level of preconceived, prejudicial thought. What kind of mystical power does this lovely, young, woman, posses? While continually seeking, the allusive forces of knowledge, truth and wisdom, though higher education, she still finds the time to share with others. These are but a few of the many truly wonderful traits of Ronita, a natural-born leader, a dedicated, co-worker, and friend.

Relentlessly devoted, to dispelling the countless myths and deceptions, that's held the masses imprisoned and void of truth. Throughout the generations, the hope and inspiration of our people, has been the elegance, and radiance of this type of beauty and glory. The captivating fragrance that eternally emanates from the very soul of such an exquisitely, priceless flower continues to be the only true source of our pride, beauty and power.

Young lady, the wisdom and understanding in the sphere that you seek, gets closer each day, with each tic of the clock, and with each new victory.

The Day Makenzie Came From Heaven

The grandmother and a great grandmother, women from two different generations, pacing back-and-forth intensely, nervously, await a word: reporting the good news. Thoughts too infinite to write down on this single sheet of paper, rush from the altar of the soul, like smoke escaping from a raging fire.

Looking back through the hourglass of time, there's countless precious memories, each with its own unique story: preserved and eternally stored within the warehouse of the mind. It's like deja-vous, looking at this precious little baby girl is like looking through a mirror back at ourselves.

Our hearts fill with love, joy and pride: knowing a precious gift, called Makenzie, will be our very first. Our hearts are bowed with respect and gratitude in the presence of the Creator, for sending this healthy, precious little gift to this family, where she will be truly cared for, and loved immensely.

Makenzie, we love you so much. We, as a family, are grateful for the opportunity to love you and watch you grow. You have uniquely touched and changed our lives forever.

Thomas Paul Monday

Natural and Free

A man's success or failure in this momentary span of time, we all call life, is not necessarily always measured in the tangible and materials things that He has been able to amass. Nor do I believe that any one man's success or failure can be measured in its entirety, as a result of a single event or accomplishment.

The true success of a man's life ought to be based on the principles of sharing and caring. He that willingly shares and cares, will always affect positive change in the world and in the lives of those, they have been afforded the rare opportunity to briefly, but eternally touch.

If one could be permitted to briefly study and analyze a few of these short encounters with such an individual, you'd see a person, who possesses a very large, sensitive and giving heart. You'd notice in an instant that this person has a love for life, and enjoyed sharing it with his family, friends, and everyone else that he met. You'd also find this to be especially true with regards, to that one person who knows him better, than anyone else, his wife.

The above statements are simple, the opinions of only one man: this writer. They are however, statements of facts, which I believe can be validated or shared by all who really and truly know.

I met Russ and his wife Clarice, at a local breakfast diner, a short time ago, or so it seemed. It was at that meeting, that I first became aware of and impressed with us, a few of the many gems that enhanced his cheerful character, which flowed natural and freely, like a bubbling spring, from some vast reservoir. This reservoir has been mystically hidden and divinely sealed, somewhere deep within, what many have called, "the treasure chest of the soul."

Reflections for the Soul

My reflection in time is nothing more than a permanent abstract in the window pane of eternity that resembles precious stones quietly cast into a calm pond of priceless memories; suspended forever somewhere within the treasure chest of the soul.

I have treasured reflections that capture the eternal beauty, elegance and essence of a budding educational career, and the successful completion of numerous professional accomplishments.

We now celebrate with you the beauty and glory concluding a wonderfully professional career, covering over twenty (20) years of faithful service to kids, and the enrichment of your peers.

You have always been a team player, who was willing to roll up your sleeves to assist students, parents, co-workers, and friends in the fulfillment of their dreams and goals.

You are and always will be a precious treasure and vital part of the Challenger Family. Let the eternal roses of beauty and the perfume from its sweetness continue with you as you transition into this new phase of life.

With eternal blessing and love, Challenger PAU Family.

Thomas Paul Monday

January 22, 2004

While sitting outside, on my patio, in my favorite reclining chair: conversing, with a few co-workers and some very special friends. Reflections of gratitude and friendship began to grow, like a beacon from a lighthouse in the fog; giving directions of safety, to the ships, entering the harbor of my soul.

Sometimes, a very special person, for only a brief moment, during this spot in time, we call "reality," will cross our path in life: to leave treasures of profound wealth. Riches, that cannot be measured, or valued like gold and silver: but which would be considered just as priceless.

It's the beautiful memory of a smile and the sweetness of the heart I believe, will certainly last forever, and these will be the jewels and gems, that I'll safely store in the treasure chest of my heart.

Happy birthday on this truly very special day!

January 16, 2004

The sounds of countless birds, loudly chirping in harmony; each one, singing in its very own unique language, a song of romance and praise, noting with awe the first rays of sunlight, that enters, through that very special window, attempting to shed enough light to magnify and glorify, the true beauty found in the treasure chest of your soul.

Their singing seems to announce and signal to the entire universe, something truly special about this young lady, on this particular day. Their singing gets louder and louder with each passing moment, and with the brightness of each additional sun ray. In absolute clarity, I now understand the words of their song.

They're simply singing, good tiding, and best wishes, for today is your birthday!

Thomas Paul Monday

I'll Just Rest in Him, Until the Morning, Mabel

Tonight, while I watched television, during the evening news, the chief meteorologist reported that a huge, violent storm was headed toward the town where I lived. He was advising everyone to seek immediate shelter.

As I lay back in the comforts of my recliner, in the dark stillness of the night, my thoughts concerning the possible affects of the quick approaching storm, began to erupt violence within my spirit: to the point of nearly causing damage to many of the precious items that had been eternally secured within the treasure chest of the soul.

Quickly approaching a point of sadness, hopelessness, misery and despair, a small, still voice within my spirit began to say, "Speak to each one of these stormy thoughts." And say with boldness, "In the name of Jesus, peace be still. I am the Creator of both the heavens and Earth."

There's creative power in His spoken Word. Once, before the very foundations of the worlds were ever formed, He created light by merely saying, "Let there be light." He only has to speak, and the powerful, harsh winds that drove the sea, causing it to become violent, ceased in obedience to His command.

My Heavenly Father has exalted the name of His beloved Son, Jesus, above every name, which is named, in both the heavens and the Earth, acknowledging Him as Lord. Jesus Christ possesses the keys of death, hell, and the grave. My Lord now sits at the right hand of the Father in glory, and He makes daily intercession to the Father just on our behalf.

I Am, The Great I Am, says come unto me that are heavy-laden with pain, worry, fear and stress. Cast all of your burdens upon me, and I'll give you the rest for which you unknowingly seek. This is why Jesus was sent from The Father in Glory, to walk among humanity, offering grace and mercy, just to demonstrate The Father Eternal, Abiding Love. It was grace, mercy, and His abiding love that permitted my Lord to take all of our sins upon Himself, on a tree instead of me.

Graciously and lovingly, my Lord, voluntarily surrendered His life to death, all alone on a cross, located at a place called Calvary. Just so that we can be redeemed back to the Father, so that we, can live with Him, in paradise throughout all of the eternity.

My children without any regret, don't weep, fret, or worry about me, because you see to be absent from the body is to be in the presence of the Lord. I'll joyfully take my rest in the arms of My Lord, patiently awaiting the Resurrection of All His Sleeping Saints.

Thomas Paul Monday

George and Gracie

Reflecting back in time to a specific moment, a very special moment, and a moment, inscribed forever on the hallowed halls of eternity. My thoughts call out to anyone who will stop and are willing to listen, as I attempt to search and seek out answers, to hundreds of unanswered life queries.

My thoughts, far innumerable to count, quietly rise up like smoke from a sacred fire long ago abandoned: refusing to be extinguished, by stubbornly continuing to simmer deep down in that abyss, called the treasure chest of the soul.

In deep thought, with a heavy heart, during the quiet stillness of the night, my thoughts continue to explode like bombs, exposing the remnants of a severely damaged heart; wounded and still bleeding from the pain and sadness, concerning a host of recent uncontrollable and unforeseen events.

Thousands of thoughts run rampant and unrestrained within my head, as I lay motionless in my bed, subdued and camouflaged by that mystical, protective cover, orchestrated and produced by the quiet stillness of the night.

I have thousands of mental images and unanswered questions, concerning the future that still seeks resolution. Thoughts that trigger questions and questions that produce additional thought, all have failed to find any acceptable solutions, as to why.

You and I, two unique individuals, parallels, running alone quietly unnoticed side by side, alike in many ways and yet so very different. I truly believe, that you and I were given a single predestined encounter; an opportunity that on a specific day, we would converge at precise point in time, during the Twilight of Chance. And, meet, in hope that both our lives forever change.

Although, I still struggle through many restless and sleepless nights, my hope and prayers are to one day find a viable solution.

Thomas Paul Monday

Chunte

My thoughts, far too many to count, quietly rise up like smoke from a sacred fire long ago abandoned, refusing to be extinguished, but stubbornly continuing to simmer deep down in that abyss, called the treasure chest of the soul.

Thousands of thoughts run rampant and unrestrained within my head, as I lay motionless in my recliner, subdued and camouflaged by that mystical cover, orchestrated and produced through the stillness of the night.

Reflecting back in time to a specific moment, a very special moment, a moment, recorded forever on the hollowed scrolls of eternity my thoughts call out all that are willing to listen, attempting to search and seek out answers, to hundreds of unanswered life queries.

You and I, two unique individuals, parallels, running alone quietly unnoticed side by side, alike in many ways and yet so very different. We were given a single, predestined encounter, a meeting, that on a specific day, we (you and I) would converge at precise point in time, during the Twilight of Chance, in hope that both our lives change forever.

Thoughts that trigger questions, and questions that produce additional thought, all have failed to find an acceptable solutions, as to why? In deep thought, with a heavy heart, during the quiet stillness of the night I continue to still reflect with great concern and sadness, a host of uncontrollable and unforeseen events.

Though I've struggled, through many restless and sleepless nights, my thoughts have failed to produce any kind of positive answers. I only have thousands of additional questions, concerning the future that still seeks resolution.

The Portrait of an Angel

There is majesty and grace, vividly and clearly preserved on the canvas of my eternal soul, which depicts the elegance and glory of a loving God. It's a true portrait, of beauty, a living memorial, illuminated and bathed, in absolute love, wisdom, and beauty.

My thoughts now free once were securely restrained within the treasure chest of my spirit. Thoughts overflow in abundance, slowly drifting quietly upwards into the abyss of the night sky. My thoughts are everlasting pictures and a memorial. My thoughts continually display gratitude for all God's grace.

My thoughts, like smoke spewing from a smoldering fire, are incense of remembrance of a very special little angel, "an angel of joy and love.

This portrait continually reminds me, that it was in the form of an angel, that God one day announced, He had given His very best, "His only Son." Finally, my portraits contain, the hope, the peace and the joy, that I will, one day soon, "See my little angel again."

Thomas Paul Monday

Cortess, a Precious Gem

Looking back over that fog-covered bridge that spans that gulf we so frequently call time, which is located somewhere between heaven and Earth: my thoughts rise up in the stillness of the night.

It's like smoke seeking escape from the confines of a raging fire that burns completely out of control somewhere on the sacred altar of the eternal soul.

Way back in the day, it was only you and I. We were a pair, like a hand and a glove. You might say a true Bonnie and Clyde.

Reflecting over the sandy beaches of life, I was amazed to see only one set of footprints instead of two pair that should have been made from you and I.

My concerns and amazement was quickly put at ease, by a quiet, still voice that said, "I've been carrying both of you in the strength of My grace, mercy and eternal love."

You and I were two young, desperate souls, searching for that mystical, hidden treasure chest that was supposed to have contained those precious gem stones of love, peace and happiness.

I've now come to realize that these precious gem stones can only be harvested and kept through God's abiding, divine grace.

He has given to each living person, seeds and the opportunity to sow in the fertile soil of life for other precious souls in order to reap an abundant harvest for the kingdom.

Sherry

Deep from within, the source of all Divine and Eternal beginnings, God, the Creator of everything, met with you and gave you your earthly assignment. He breathed the precious breath of life, into the dust of your very soul, and endowed you with special qualities or gifts only befitting a princess.

Qualities, talents and gifts required for the eventual transformation into a precious, beautiful strong, Black Queen. The Creator's gift of love, involved unselfish acts of caring for others, the sharing of one's time and resources with those who are less fortunate than yourself.

God's love is the benchmark and standard, if you truly desire to affect change in the lives of those you encounter. Your unique personality is sweet, honest, and pure, therefore, whatever you do for others, truly comes from your heart. These are rare qualities that can only be found, in its basic and sweetest form, which truly represent the idea or the concept, we so call love.

My thoughts, which are far too numerous to even be listed on this single sheet of blank paper, range from "Talking Tina," to those two very special events you refer to as childbirth.

This life's sunsets will one day come to a close for me, and so let me take this opportunity now, to tell you, your mom and I, are very proud of you, our firstborn and only daughter.

Our prayer is that the eternal God of Heaven, continue to guide you and bless you with his tender mercy.

Thomas Paul Monday

Lamar

While relaxed and resting within the comforts of a newly-purchased lazy boy,

I began to reflect back to the days of my youth, in what I suppose was a feeble attempt to recapture and somehow magically retain sacred images of the days, times and events of the long distant past.

Thoughts and images from my youth quickly began to fill the sanctuary of my soul: like smoke forcibly escaping upwards into the sky from the confines of a fire, now raging completely out-of-control.

Peering through the stained glass window of my soul at the various items of importance that I had stored in the heart, I desperately wanted to see the real me.

I became confused and somewhat perplexed when I saw you.

The thought occurred to me, as if sunlight had suddenly illuminated a dark room.

"This is who I once was, and one day you'll be looking in your own mirror at me.

"Vanity, vanity, vanity! Son, it's all vanity!"

Son, plan and work hard during the day, because the daylight will surely surrender its power like a thief in the night.

My son, take heed and remember that this life is temporal, like vapor appearing for a brief moment, only to then disappear. Please take time to appreciate the peace and beauty of each new day, as you enjoy the sweet fragrance of the flowers along the way.

Son, don't stress too much about tomorrow, have faith in the God of all creation, in the days of your youth, knowing with total confidence that He will continue to bless and keep you.

Thomas Paul Monday

Milton

When this life's evening sun starts to go dim, and eventually fade to black, allow me to look back to the beginning and proudly reflect. Allow the joy of my thoughts to swell up in my fledgling spirit like smoke quickly escaping from a sacred fire that has engulfed and now completely consumes the remains of a sacrifice abandoned on the altar of the soul.

Let the sweet fragrance and pride from my reflective thoughts, ascend upwards towards the heavens, and be eternally recorded in the books of life, as a promise kept, good job, well done! When I prayed, I prayed for a son, just like you, one that would carry my name, a son that would be bone-of-my-bone and flesh-of-my-flesh.

I prayed to God for a son just like you. I prayed for a son just like you, one that would love the Lord and fear God. I prayed to God. He heard my prayer and he blessed me with you. You're my son, and that's living proof, that the eternal God of the heavens does answer prayers and make dreams come true.

May God continue to bless and keep you safely in the arms of His eternal love.

Kevin

While peering through diminishing eyes, at a silent camouflage image of a stranger, quietly looking back at me from the opposite side of that hidden reflective surface called time, countless thoughts and emotions began to explode within the sacred confines of the treasure chest in my soul.

Abstract thoughts of gray and black, began to rise within my spirit like smoke swiftly escaping from a raging fire, out-of-control somewhere deep within that eternal abyss.

Realizing the finality of life and the preciousness of each moment, I began to reflect on the fact that the camouflage stranger in the mirror by some weird twist in reality might really be me.

The loving, sweet, calming, familiar voice of a mother long ago, gone home to be with the Lord, quietly whispered in my subconscious ear, "Son, just keep on living. You'll understand it all bye and bye. Life will teach you a thing or two, and what was will be because we didn't come here to stay always."

While gazing intently at the distorted reflective stranger in the mirror, he acknowledges my newly-discovered revelation with a shake of the head and wide distinctive grin. The young, strong boy of my youth had become frail and old.

I realized that there are other things, much more important besides acquiring fame, or storehouses full of silver and gold. "Son, remember the Creator in the days of your youth, for it is, He that will bless you, and keep you even to the preserving of your soul."

May the eternal God of heaven bless and keep you always.

Thomas Paul Monday

Brian

The sharp, young spring ran constantly in a condition that many would describe as being, "much too light." Flashes of brilliance would on occasion, sporadically light the darkened chamber that contained a mind that many believed to be long ago abandoned, and void of any useful content.

The street that once developed instants of self-preservation and self-defense, had over the years, became the primary theme and a major part of the daily scheme to run one's own program. Too many have tried to tie a reason to a possible cause, which may have brought about results and the presence of this mysterious effect.

There are those who have said, "It was the drugs." Others believe, it's from being locked up too long, while, still others say it's the results of not being locked up long enough. Finally, there are still those who openly shake their heads in utter amazement and truthfully admit that they don't know. Then, it always becomes crystal clear when all of the game-playing and noise has stopped, and when the atmosphere of violence and confusion has been exchanged for one of peace.

There in the center, if you look carefully, with a kind of innocent looking smile, you'll still find Brian.

Mechael,
You're Daddy's Little Girl

Your arrival from heaven in the precious arms of an angel was a very special and joyful event. My thoughts and emotions surrounding your arrival are too numerous to even begin to write down on this simple sheet of paper.

Thousands of thoughts, feeling and emotions, continuously erupt in my head like exploding bombs, leaving behind clouds of dust filled smoke. Thoughts that fill the night sky, with sacred smoke that quickly rise from a raging fire that's consuming a sacrifice, abandoned on the altar of the soul.

Thoughts that appear for only a brief moment and then disappear forever into that abyss called eternity. Mechael, I'm so proud of you. I'm proud to be called your dad, and I'm even more proud to call you, daddy's little girl. I wait patiently to hold you and protect you. I want to teach you about the love and the goodness of God. You have an extended family that truly love and want you to have the very best.

Mechael you deserve the very best, because you are and always will be daddy's little girl.

Thomas Paul Monday

Wishing You the Very Best

Jan, there are so many precious moments and memories of you, until I really don't know quite, just where to begin. Reflections in time, like the ripping effect of waves on a quiet pond: reacting to the sudden impact of a stone, now engulfs a career that currently spans over 19 years of faithful service.

The rise and beauty of this professional career now successfully culminates in the splendor of a wonderful sunset. Each of us has captured permanently in our hearts precious moments, which has been suspended; in that brief, abstract, spot, located somewhere in eternity, which was so often refer to as "time."

Tic-Toc-Tic-Toc the second hand of the clock continues relentlessly, just where does all of the time really go? Like the quiet beauty of a leisurely flowing stream, on course to some predetermined destination, downstream: close to the center of our hearts, we your co-workers and friends, over these past 19 years, have seen one another through the thick and the thin.

Jan, even though you're retiring, it doesn't change a thing; you'll always be an important part of the Challenger PAU Family.

Jan, we all really love you, and wish you the very, very best.

Daddy's Little Girl

Daddy's little girl. My thoughts are forever, all about you: like smoke rising silently into the night air. I'm a lucky man. God blessed me with a beautiful little angel. My thoughts are special about you. God blessed me with a beautiful little angel. I'm really a very lucky man.

Thomas Paul Monday

Aliya

The Creator of the universe decided to send another gift to earth, a precious, little baby girl named Aliya. Searching for the perfect set of parents, God selected your mom and dad as the proud recipients, who would shower this priceless little bundle, with an abundance of love. His only requirements for your parents were that, they always be there for you, as spiritual guides to demonstrate the Creator's eternal love and mercy for humanity.

Your parents are to remind you that you are on temporary loan to them, and that they are to teach you about the Creator's laws, His mercy and His love. If you honor your parents, your days on Earth will be long.

We celebrated your anticipated arrival with an abundance of fanfare, laughter and joy, as you entered this world with a special angelic escort. My thoughts and emotions, concerning your arrival, are too numerous to be contained on this simple sheet of paper.

Countless, emotional thoughts, producing multiple smoke-filled explosions within the treasure chest of my soul, quickly rise into the night sky, seeking escape from the raging fire now burning out-of-control, somewhere deep within the abyss.

With love and thanksgiving, we invite you to live forever within our hearts. We look forward to being a vital part of your life, as we watch you grow up into adulthood.

We offer continual prayers, for daily deposit on the Creator's sacred altar of mercy, located in heaven for His protection, health, and eternal blessings.

Precious Poetic Moments

Congratulation, Mrs. Coffee

It's really a rare occasion, during times like these, that one is able to encounter someone special like you,

Special people like you, are like diamonds, very rare and priceless.

Someone like you, who really cares.

Someone like you, who's cool.

Someone like you, who's fair.

Someone like you, who's always willing to listen.

Mrs. Coffee, you really are the greatest. All of us, minors and staff in Camp Smith, offer our best wishes and congratulations. We wish you the very best, wherever you go.

We know that with your personality and success we will certainly follow you in everything that you set your heart and mind to do.

Thomas Paul Monday

Phil, Ask Me If I Care

It was 3:30 in the morning, when I slowly awoke, relaxed and completely laid back, within the secure confines of my brown, leather recliner. My MGD was still clutched firmly within the palm of my hand. Tunes from some of my favorite songs, reminiscent of days long, long past, surround me, and keep playing over and over again in my head.

Cautiously, slowly, opening one eye at-a-time, my vision adjusts to the brightness of a newly-installed, flashing yellow neon light. Countless thoughts move, aimlessly to-and-fro within the abstract boundary of my mind: as if I'm, eternally dazed by some unknown mystical force. These thoughts, far, far too many to even commence to identify or count, are mental slaves and prisoners, held as permanent sober inhabitants of the mind, due to the lack of common sense and sound reasoning.

Phil therefore, I must conclude, that the joy of real freedom like an Artesian Spring, comes only from that abyss that lay deep, within the treasure chest of the eternal soul. And so when asked if I care about anything else, I must truly confess, that I really don't!

Genevieve

God really blessed me, with a family and a special little angel like you.

Daddy's little girl. Thinking about you and your mom. Wow! I'm a lucky man. My thoughts rise, like smoke rising silently into the night air.

My thoughts are, all about the future, watching and looking at you, as you grow up. My heart: Daddy's little girl. My thoughts will always and forever be all about you.

Thomas Paul Monday

Noah

Listening to the soft, soothing and relaxing sounds of smooth jazz, while resting within the comforts of my Easy Boy™ recliner, during the quiet, stillness of the night, I began to reflect back on various aspects and events that had occurred within my life over the years. As I continued to meditate on those aspects and events, floodgates of emotions were opened, inundating my spirit with countless memories, of just how good God has been to my family and me.

I'm eternally grateful to the God of the heavens, and the Creator of the universe for His continuous expressions of blessings of love. There is an old spiritual song, entitled, "I Get a Blessing Every day." I believe just like the flood that was mentioned in the Bible, which covered the entire Earth, my newest grandchild, Noah Jones Whitley, has also managed to flood and completely submerge, the very treasure chest of my soul, as a fresh example of God's ability to still create expressions of His divine and eternal love.

Oh Lord, You are God Almighty, from everlasting to everlasting. You alone, created both the heavens and the Earth, please accept my prayers of thanksgiving, as an acceptable burnt offering for your continued gifts of blessings and mercy, Amen.

Yvette,
Angelic Beauty in Any Language

Several nights ago, when I was relaxing within the comforts of my Easy Boy™ recliner, and listening to the soft, soothing sounds of jazz from my stereo, wave-after-wave of countless, thoughts and fond memories of very special people in my life began to invade the sanctuary of my spirit.

Thoughts and fond memories, too numerous to count or list, rose up into the night sky of my spirit like sacred smoke, slowly escaping from a fire, yet eternally burning on the altar of my soul. Over the years, you've shown me innumerable instances of kindness and have given me tons of very, sound practical advice. I'm reminded of the comfort that often came from that reassuring, and infectiously beautiful smile.

The beauty and security of our professional friendship has evolved over the course of several years to the point that I can now say with very strong conviction; I consider you a true friend. Thoughts and memories of our professional friendship will be everlasting. Each thought and precious memory, void of all doubt or any reservation, shall be forever stored within the memorial treasure chest of my soul. Yvette, you truly are a valued co-worker, and a precious friend.

The beauty of your smile, your words of wisdom and personality lead me to believe, that angels can still be found in only two places: heaven and right here on planet Earth. The descriptive word for an angel in any language is still "Yvette."

Thomas Paul Monday

George

Asleep within the arms of death, there is rest and peace in the sacred bosom of eternity. I recall the parable of the rich man and Lazarus; there really is an abyss that separates the living from the dead. My thoughts, once securely stored within the treasure chest of the soul now float unhindered upwards: like smoke escaping from the remnants of a once raging fire, now abandoned and left smoldering.

I now understand, how short life actually is and like a vapor, does appear as a brief, undetectable micro-speck on that timeline called "forever." The pride of life with all its glory and splendor that one works so hard to possess, quickly dissolves and eventually does cease to exist.

Roses given as tokens of love are always best received by the intended recipient, when their fragrance and beauty are fully appreciated through the senses of sight, touch or smell. If I could relive just a few seconds in that brief abstract called life, one of the first things I'd do, is apologize for not being there when you really needed me.

I would say that I was sorry, for being too macho to hug and hold you. I'd tell you, "How much I love you," and the enormous amount of pride it gave me simply just to call you dad.

Please always remember me.

In Memory of
A Wonderful and Loving Son-In-Law

Beautiful and eternal images of a wonderful, loving, son-in-law are far too numerous to even calculate. During this time of loss and sadness, countless thoughts and fond memories continue to ascend like smoke into the quiet stillness of the night sky.

Memories and mental images which rise spontaneously are joyfully rehearsed and replayed from infinite selections stored within the treasure chest of my soul. Reflecting upon this brief ripple in space we so often refer to as time, I'm reminded of innumerable moments and occasions, filled with love and happiness.

I am grateful for the privilege to have known you, and the opportunity to have witnessed the joy and happiness, which you brought into our lives, by just being such an important part of this family.

Anthony, although I've told you, so many, many times before, this time, it's for the record, so that the whole world will also know,

I love you, and you'll always be my Son-In-Law.

Love always Mom, Elizabeth.

Thomas Paul Monday

Barbara

There are thousands of final thoughts running rampant and unrestrained within my head, as this year slowly comes to an end that will forever be stored in the treasure chest of my soul. Laying quietly and motionless in my bed, my thoughts are subdued and camouflaged by that mystical, protective cover; orchestrated and produced by the quiet stillness of the night.

You and I were assigned a single predestined appointment, a mystical encounter, and a very rare and precious opportunity to meet each other, at a precise moment in time, during the Twilight of Chance, in hope that each of our lives would be changed forever. You and I were and still are two very unique individuals, with lives that parallel the one another, unnoticed, quietly running side-by-side, alike in many ways, and yet so very different.

Reflecting back in time to that specific moment, a very special moment, and a moment, etched forever on one of the hollowed pages. In the book called Life, my thoughts called out to anyone who was willing to stop and listen, as I made a desperate attempt to search and seek out answers, to hundreds of unanswered life queries.

In deep thought, with a heavy heart, during the quiet stillness of the night, my thoughts continue to explode like bombs, exposing the remnants of a severely-damaged heart, wounded and still bleeding. Thoughts that trigger questions, and questions that produce additional thought, have failed to find any acceptable solutions, as to why?

Dazed and confused from years of neglect, there still remains much evidence of all past pain: untold sadness, from a host of recent uncontrollable, and unforeseen events. I have thousands of mental images and unanswered questions, concerning the future that still seeks resolution.

My desire and prayers are that as I struggle, fighting restlessness, physical trails and countless sleepless nights that I shall eventually prevail through His Divine intervention and grace.

Although my thoughts, are far too many to count, they continue to quietly rise up like smoke from a sacred fire long ago abandoned: refusing to never be extinguished, by stubbornly continuing to simmer deep down in that abyss, called the treasure chest of the soul.

Thomas Paul Monday

Eva

Eva, deep within the treasure chest of my soul are priceless memories. Indelible memories like captivating fragrance of perfume are eternal and full of life. They continue forever, unhindered by any physical or natural law. They are able to transcend the abyss of both time and space.

The beauty of your smile and the sparkle in your eyes like smoke rising, quietly and slowly into the night sky, are but brief moments, suspended forever in time, reflecting all that was, and everything that eventually will be.

They remain safely and tenderly stored, in the very essence of what we so fondly, call the treasure chest of the soul. Reflections, like the sweetness of sugar, warm the human heart, and radiate continually beauty and love for life.

We'll always remember with a smile, just how much you've truly touched our lives, as a humanitarian, co-worker, and friend.

A Reflection in Time,
In Loving Memory of Erma

While thinking and reflecting, during the quiet, stillness of the night, about Mrs. Erma V. E. and the beauty of her life, there are not enough words to accurately describe all of the beauty that was actually stored in the treasure chest of this precious soul.

How does one formulate enough nouns, verbs and adjectives in one sentence? How can you portray the security of a hug, beauty of that special smile, or the warmth that comes from the tender loving care that only a mother could give to a child that's sick? Life is like smoke, rising slowly into the air from a smoldering fire. It's visible for only a brief moment, and then quietly vanished, leaving behind forever in silence, all of this world's heartaches and pain.

In portraits of love and beauty, you've touched our lives in so many ways, with countless examples and memories that will be cherished forever.

Thomas Paul Monday

That Early Morning Flight,
In Loving Memory of Carmen

My children, don't worry or fret about me. My life like smoke released into the early morning air from a slow, smoldering fire is a reflection of change. I've finally left the confines and physical limitations of this world behind. My soul has been released and set free to take flight and soar, beyond the gravitational pull of every mortal man.

I'm finally free to journey to a land, completely void of all heartache and physical pain. I can now live throughout eternity in peace, harmony and in perfection without conflict. My children, don't worry about me. I've taken that early morning flight.

I have the promise, and the guaranteed assurance, that for me everything is going to be all right. My fare has been paid for in full, by the one-and-only man who could guarantee such a safe, first class seat, on that Early Morning Flight.

The Legacy of this Man!
In Loving Memory of Mr. Robert

I remember, yesterday as if it were today. I'm always thinking and reminiscing. Reflecting back on the countless memories of yesterday that continually flow, totally free and unhindered from the very depths of the soul. My thoughts like smoke from a nearly-extinguished fire, rise silently into the stillness of the air and quietly vanish.

I remember and smile, at your words of wisdom, concerning many of the issues of this life, that you and I so often talked about. As a co-worker, and a friend, you've been an example of how charity and love can and does make a difference, in the lives of all we meet.

Even though your present journey, has removed you from the confines of this physical world, I know you're still hard at-work, renewing old friendships, making new ones, being gracious, and as an industrious volunteer, just willing to help out wherever you can.

Bob, this is dedicated to you and your loving memory forever as I reflect upon the legacy you've given us.

Thomas Paul Monday

In the Mirror of the Heart
Dedicated to Jardine Charles

The love I feel is like reflections in time and space. The images that I see when I look into the mirror are not really of me. My mind contemplates reflecting quietly in the stillness of the night reclined and relaxed in the comfort of my easy chair.

My thoughts rise up into the night sky and slowly disappear: like smoke escaping from a fire, which had once been contained. Looking into the mirror I can't help but see and remember all of the love and sacrifices you did to make our lives just a little easier.

Looking into the mirror at the image of myself and at everything that I've been able to accomplish for myself in this life, I can't help but see you also standing there with me, giving me words of wisdom and encouragement. I see a strong, tall Black man standing proud, with enough love and beauty, flowing freely from the treasure chest of the soul for each of us.

The joy I feel, which I'll cherish forever, comes from reminiscing, and knowing that each time I look into the mirror of my heart, you'll always be there.

Sugar Doesn't Come Any Sweeter

Jan, here you are, you've finally arrived at your destination: retirement, that port of call for which we all strive and set sail, when we first start our professional careers. While thinking about you, lots of thoughts and fond memories began to flow through the treasure chest of the heart.

Thoughts and memories too numerous to even count, began to rise up into the stratosphere of the soul like smoke quietly, but quickly escaping from the consuming reaches of a very hot fire.

In Rodeos, it's ride 'em cowgirl! Don't turn lose that bucking beast 'till you get your dollars' worth of time! The fun, laughter, and the sweetness of the music, all have finally come to a complete stop.

Then and only then, may you give that young man, in uniform an opportunity to take your boarding pass. Jan, sugar doesn't come any sweeter than you. It's been wonderful for these past nineteen years: one great big party, even though we've all gone through some pretty rough times, it still has been one, long wonderful party.

Jan, all of us, as part of the Challenger PAU Family, love you and wish you nothing but the very, very best.

Thomas Paul Monday

Hannah

How does one, unselfishly start to share with the world, the true value of all of the wonderful and invaluable gifts, which we have received from you over the years? The thoughts and memories of these gifts are eternally stored deep within the treasure chest of the soul. Infinite thought and precious memories continue daily to float upwards within my spirit from the confines of the heart, like a sweet fragrance released from an unsealed bottle of a very popular perfume.

It is especially significant on a very special occasion like today, that these strong thoughts and emotions have an even greater meaning. It is because of this annual day, that we all joyfully momentarily, pause to celebrate, give thanks and pay homage to you. You see, it is this special day, which denotes your beginning, in this brief span of eternity on planet Earth; we call "life."

The most valued and priceless of all of the gifts, which I have eternally stored deep within the treasure chest of my soul has been that one special gift, which you gave to each of your children, and that is, "the Gift of Life."

Mother this is your day, Happy Birthday, from all of us.

Mama Clara

A host of angelic messengers were quietly dispatched from heaven today, riding swiftly on the calm winds of the early morning's air, being specifically instructed to personally escort one of His beloved children.

Mama Clara home for a celebration of eternal peace and rest; after being blessed to obtain, nine score and three (93) years of what we call human life. When I was notified of the sad, devastating news, prompted numerous floodgates of emotions and fond memories of Mama Clara: contained within my spirit to be released, in a futile attempt to find eternal solitude within the treasure chest of my soul.

Although I'm sad, I find comfort in knowing that to be absent from the body, is to be in the presence of the Lord, and that the Lord promised that He would never leave nor forsake any of His children. All of my thoughts, my love and admiration for Mama Clara cannot be contained on this simple sheet of paper. They are, however, exploding within my spirit like bombs being ignited on a battlefield.

It is Mama Clara, who took me into her home as a foster child, at the age of 12, showing me love and providing protection. It was Mama Clara, who taught me countless life lessons such as; how to cook; sew; behave like a young lady; have respect for my elders; and for myself as a strong Black woman. It was Mama Clara who instilled in me the concept to work hard to accomplish my goals and dreams.

Mama Clara was a beautiful, living example, who demonstrated that even without a college education, while working at a dry cleaners' and as a church nurse, that if you possessed faith and trusted in God, all things were possible. Mama Clara, I love you. I appreciate your loving me like a daughter, and I'm grateful for everything you've done for me.

Mama, now celebrate and enjoy your rest in the loving arms of Jesus. I'll see you again one glorious day. Love always, Yvette.

Thomas Paul Monday

Take a Chance with Me

I don't know if I have the academic ability to accurately verbalize just how much you mean to me. I wish it were possible for you to obtain a one-hour tour pass. During that one hour, you would be allowed to visit and observe first-hand all of the countless, priceless memories of you that are eternally stored within the treasure chest of my soul.

I went to the Webster Dictionary in hopes of finding a definition equal to the essence of the love that I have for you. I had hoped to find a meaning that would capture the absolute beauty and pure perfection in one or two sentences.

I had also hoped to find a word that defines a scientific term and yet easily explains in plain layman terminology, just how you make me feel physically and emotionally whenever I'm around you.

How do you explain multiples knots in one's chair, or the inability to speak in complete sentences, without using such phrases as, "Wow, awe-, yeah buddy," just a name a few.

Is there really an explanation, when you've hoped and prayed, and one day, you finally awake in a brand new and exciting reality, in which your wildest dreams, has actually come true?

My dreams and hopes became my reality, the day we met and I found myself freed from the abyss, hopelessly, passionately, head-over-heels, in love with you. Thank you for taking a chance with me.

Precious,
A Priceless Little Survivor

Countless thoughts and prayers of faith and hope ascend through the portals of heaven, right to the very throne of our Heavenly Father: and with a smile He hears our every prayer. The sweet fragrance from the prayers of thanksgiving, continually rise toward the heavens from the altar of the souls of the children of God like eternal smoke, silently escaping from sacred fires, thanking our Father with the fruits of our mouth, for His abundance in love and mercy.

Most of all, our prayers, thank our Heavenly Father for the best gift of all, His son, Jesus Christ, The Living Word. Jesus' words resonate deep within the Christian's spirit to suffer not the little children to come unto me, for such is the Kingdom of Heaven. There, they behold the Father's face continually and precious are they in His sight.

God sent His Word. The Word became flesh and dwelled among us, and we beheld His Glory. Then, the Word healed them of all their infirmities. The Word, never changes. For the Word, is Love. The Word is the same yesterday, today, and forever.

Precious God loves you, and you'll always be very, very precious in His sight.

Thomas Paul Monday

It's Official

Sitting in my recliner, anxious excitedly waiting, anticipating with awe and wonder sensing each passing moment in time that reverberates from the second hand as it makes it way around the face of the clock.

Tic-Toc-Tic-Toc.

How much longer can I, must I, be forced to wait, before I receive that special call? My thoughts of my little girl, now an adult, married and soon Tic-Toc-Tic-Toc, a proud mother, with a son of her very own. My thoughts of joy, laughter and limitless memories are eternal, with each one covering a brief moment in reality that we so fondly refer to as "Time."

These thoughts, which engulf yesterday, today and, even tomorrow, rise silently, like smoke, from a smoldering fire, into the stillness of the night air, slowly disappearing. Realizing that you live just one or two states away, offers me a little comfort. And yet, in my soul, it is still feels like some strange, foreign and distant land.

Like any proud parent, I get really get excited and happy, when I hear that Michael (Wolfgang) and you are doing well: in love and together, supporting one another as a family. In unity, you'll be able to take on and defeat each and every adversity.

At 2:10 a.m., January 7, 2004, I finally received that special call notifying me, not to worry, that it's official, I'm a new Grandpa, and that Wolfgang was born a fine, healthy baby boy.

God Sent a Very Precious Little Girl, Layla

Strong feelings of love, joy and pride, swell up within me: like steam, and air-filled bubbles being forcefully released from a newly-open underwater volcanic crevice somewhere deep on the ocean's floor. The Creator of the universe, and the giver of all perfect gifts, once again has granted permission for another one of His precious little angels, to leave the confines of heaven, come to Earth and dwell among mortal men.

Looking through the windows of the spirit at the volumes of personal, precious memories, preserved and eternally stored within the treasure chest of my soul, it's like deja-vous looking at you, is like looking at me.

Appearing in living color, like the way that God promised Noah, He would always remember, by placing the rainbow in the sky after a sudden rain, a newly married couple reaffirming their vows. Their head's bowed with respect and gratitude in the presence of the Creator, for sending this special little gift.

This precious gift of life has been blessed and sent from the Creator of the universe, so that she in turn will be a blessing to others and touch the lives of many. In the window I see two loving parents, tenderly kissing their precious little angel, as she lay resting peacefully, cradled in her father two massive masculine hands, whispering repeatedly in unison.

We Love You Layla

We Love You Layla

Thomas Paul Monday

Allen David

How do I find the right combination of descriptive words, to accurately describe the life of Allen David, and the affect that he had on the lives of all that knew him? Allen's life, like a vapor existed for only a brief moment, somewhere within that vague, and infinite abstract called eternity.

While reflecting on a friendship that quickly developed over a period of several months, I began to recall countless acts of kindness and a genuine concern for others. Collectively, my own personal thoughts and memories are far too numerous to be contained on a simple single sheet of paper. These thoughts, amplified by a power of 10, rise upwards from the treasure chest of the soul, like smoke from a smoldering fire, into the abyss of the night sky and there slowly disappear.

Allen's life, like, the psychology term, "The Butterfly Effect," is a living testimonial of friendship, courage, dedication and professional mentoring. Allen's life also accurately illustrates, just how much one individual over a span of 73 years, can touch and change the lives of so many.

It has truly been an honor, a privilege and a blessing to have known Allen David, as a mentor, a co-worker, and a very good friend.

My Loving Dad
Eldrew

Thoughts and mental images of my loving father are far too numerous to even begin to analyze. Memories and mental images rise spontaneously, cheerfully rehearsed and replayed from infinite selections stored within the treasure chest of my eternal soul.

During this loss and time of sadness, countless thoughts and fond memories continue to ascend like smoke into the quiet stillness of the night sky. Reflecting back through this brief ripple in space we so often refer to as "time," I'm reminded of innumerable moments and occasions, filled with lots of laughter, love and happiness.

I remember as a child, the hard work, dedication, and the responsibilities that rested on your shoulders from; being a husband, father, and a provider. Daddy, although I've told you, so many, many times before, this time, it's for the record, so that the whole world will also know:

I love you, and I'm glad you're my Dad.

Thomas Paul Monday

Audrey, Here We Are Again

The other day, after we had that brief talk, I tried to remember exactly when our professional friendship really first began. Thoughts of those very first memorable encounters began to rise up within my spirit, like smoke slowly escaping into the quiet stillness of the night, from some sacred eternal flames, located only on the altar of the soul. After 43-plus years of faithful, academic service to students and their parents as a professional educator, how do you really, just say good-bye?

Fondly, I still remember, on various occasions how you so lovingly would share infinite words of encouragement and wisdom. They freely flowed from your many years of personal, real-life experiences and professional growth. The word, Love, is the one term that best describes your 43-plus years of professional, educational service.

The love for teaching: continually stimulating the minds of students through the development of positive and inquisitive thought. Love, dedicates itself to the growth of confidence, self-esteem and personal empowerment. Love never gets tired of sharing with any student, the gift of academic enlightenment.

Audrey, here you are at the sunset of a very long and successful career. This is another opportunity to display and share with others in a different setting: your zeal for life, which is a direct result of the love you have gained from the sacred gift to teach others.

It's the first day of enrollment in another academic school in life and you have begun reading the first chapter of a brand new book, therefore, just for the joy, that comes from the love you have for teaching others, simply say, "Here We Go Again!"

Precious Poetic Moments

Happy Birthday, Chemina

The other day I had the opportunity to be a part of the staff's birthday celebration for a very special lady. My thoughts of the event are probably too numerous to put down on paper, but nonetheless, the celebration left an everlasting impression, showing just how much this individual was appreciated and so fondly thought of.

In retrospect, my thoughts of the celebration was like water, gushing from some artesian well high in the mountains, which then began swiftly running its natural coarse downhill. My thoughts are like water cascading over waterfall, gathering for several brief moments in a large pool of remembrance and then slowly disappearing unrestrained downstream.

The lady, whose birthday celebration I observed, is truly blessed and is a blessing to others. My thoughts and observations of this celebration also attest to the fact, that there are indeed angelic beings still among us, clothed in human form.

Patience and careful observation will reveal their true identity. Watch for a beautiful smile and endless acts of kindness. As I listened closely to this lady, I heard continual words of praise and thanksgiving but I couldn't catch her name.

Finally someone said, "Happy Birthday, Chemina"

Thomas Paul Monday

Nelda, A Living Portrait of Beauty Revealed

Patches of diverse colors are permanently and artistically arranged on a living canvas, reflecting the beauty, skills and natural talents, that some call, a "Gift," My thoughts, concerning this precious living portrait, are like the endless brush strokes that it contains: far, far too infinite to even attempt to write down on this one, single sheet of paper.

Countless, priceless memories rise up into the night sky, like smoke quickly escaping from a sacred fire, burning on the eternal altar of the soul. This majestic living canvas is revealed and concealed, within a three-dimensional abstract that bridges the abyss of time and space.

A tapestry of living pictures of color, eternally captured on canvas: depicting various titles and meanings. The canvas reveals a wife, mother, friend, extremely talented artist, and a woman of class. Copies and authentic replicas of this mesmerizing portrait have been reproduced, traded and sold in hundreds of galleries.

However, there is only one original, and that one very special Portrait of Living Beauty, is called "Nelda."

A Reflective Fragrance, Billie

The sweet fragrance that radiates from the perfume of incalculable thoughts and priceless memories, continually float upwards from the storehouse, within the abyss of my soul into the atmosphere of the night sky and silently disappear.

I had to childishly smile as I began to reflect back to numerous events and cherished memories suspended forever as a moment of time somewhere within the abyss called eternity.

How do you accurately calculate or place a value on the contributions that you have made to an innumerable amount of students, co-workers, friends and other professional peers? My reflections that are too numerous to even begin to count will always stand as a living testimonial to your academic growth, professional excellence and a true love for helping kids.

May the Lord bless and keep you, as you enter this new and exciting chapter in your life.

Love always, Your Challenger School Family.

Thomas Paul Monday

The Coach

The practice session, started off just like any other normal sunny day I guess, except for some new guy that seemed to be all over the field at the same time, like a traffic cop, carefully guiding, encouraging, directing, and giving out instructions to ensure that the flow of traffic on the field would continue to move smoothly.

Sitting quietly in the bleachers, I watched and listened intensely to every word that the short, bearded man, wearing the fisherman's hat spoke. I became profoundly impressed with the man's knowledge, enthusiasm, and love for what he truly enjoyed doing, motivating and challenging athletes to be the best in whatever sport they were actively participating in.

Inquisitively, I asked several students sitting near me, "Who is the short, bearded white guy wearing the fisherman's hat?" They replied almost in unison, "They call him 'The coach, that's Coach Stevens.'"

In retrospect, over the years, I've enjoyed listening to numerous success stories of athletes that you've coached, who have gone on to very successful, professional athletic careers.

When you speak of Coach Robinson, honoring and remembering what he accomplished while he was Head Football Coach at Grambling State University, it is a living testimonial of the love, praise and, respect that he's given out to others. Your dedication and hard work over the years has gained you the same well-deserved respect from countless family members, students, co-workers and friends.

In the quiet stillness of the night, my thoughts of you, your family, your numerous words of wisdom, and our friendship over these past several years, are too numerous to be contained within the confines of that abstract called, "Time."

Quietly overflowing the sacred banks is a new, refreshing water that was retrained through fear and pain, but now gives renewed strength and hope to a once, parched fertile valley.

Coach, you've given a precious gift to the countless lives that you've touched, helping them to identify the true riches of joy and peace, which had been lying dormant, hidden within the treasure chest of the soul.

Thomas Paul Monday

A Celebration of Life, James I'll Keep the Faith, Until We Meet Again

The other day while I sat quietly, in a lawn chair on the beach, I was struck with awe and wonder as I observed the sun surrendering the last of its brilliant rays of light, to the swiftly encroaching dark stillness of the night. Thoughts of you, a very, very close and one of my best friends, began to rise up within me, like smoke slowly escaping from a fire that had just started to consume a sacrifice left unattended on the sacred altar of my soul.

It really doesn't seem to have been that long ago, when you left behind this old world of heartache, sickness and pain. You've pulled off that old mortal, corruptible suit, and exchanged it for one that's incorruptible. This regenerated, tailored suit best reflects and resembles the surrounding decor of your new, eternal, celestial home.

Frequently, I look at old pictures and replay countless memories in my head that capture the brief moments of allotted time you spent with your family and a host of friends, while you still lived in that old house built with mortal clay.

My old friend, although I miss your smiling face and all the good times we had, I won't allow myself to become too sad, because I realize, you're at peace: free of pain and now reside in a much, much better place.

I'll keep the faith, until we meet again.

The Light House of My Soul, Jack

A lone ship containing a very precious cargo, which before the very foundations of the world were ever formed, divinely set sail, leaving that sacred celestial port called Eternal Glory. Within the very bowels of the ship in a storage room, a deposit was made on my behalf, for my safety, peace, and eternal security.

It lay dormant and secure, deep within the treasure chest of my soul, waiting for the day, that its rightful owner would present the key to open the lock. This old ship of mine constructed of temporal, mortal clay has been tossed to and fro, by the violent stormy waves, spanning the oceans of this old life.

But the captain of my ship of has made me a promise: despite the rough trials and tribulations that I may encounter on the rough stormy seas of this old life, to one day safely bring me to the Harbor of Eternal Rest.

The Captain of my ship, of whom I put all of my faith, hope and trust, is King Jesus. He is the King of Kings and Lord of Lords. He is the Creator of both the heavens and the Earth. He is the Great I Am. His light is the Glory of heaven and He is the light of this world. It is in King Jesus and Him alone that I can boldly boast with confidence, to bring this old weary ship safely into Heaven's Port.

The only requirement that my Lord and my King ask of me is to spread His Word, so that other lost souls might also find their way, by steering their ships towards the Glory of His light, as it brightly shines through the windows of *"The Light House of My Soul."*

Thomas Paul Monday

The Sun Will Continue to Shine, After Every Rough, Stormy, Rainy Day, Charlotte & Lucky

The Creator of both the heavens and the Earth gave his eternal word in the form of a visual promise, which was fulfilled when He created the rainbow. He then, lovingly placed it in the sky for everyone to see. It's as a solemn reminder of God's endless love, mercy and grace. It's truly reassuring, to see that brightly colored rainbow, stretched like a curtain across a vast sea of dark-colored, rain-soaked clouds, which had slowly began to form, but now suddenly, and forcefully have completely filled the sky. The dark, quiet night sky then began to erupt with deafening sounds of thunder, with blinding flashes of lightening, all followed by a sudden deluge of enormous drops of falling rain

The rich variations in color is another one of God's natural laws or promises, that's openly displayed with awe and wonder, divinely representing the entirety of all humanity, the final crowing jewel, to make the rainbow eternally complete. The Rainbow was placed in the sky as a visual reminder, that God is always present and that He is always willing to love, to forgive, to strengthen and to even heal the devastating effects of lives that have been shattered into countless pieces from the hopeless fleeing memories of yesterday.

Have you ever stopped to consider the fact, that after every rainstorm, the sun has never forgotten or simply refused to shine? Have you ever been left permanently in total darkness? Are you surrounded by the enemies, of sadness, misery, loneliness, heartache and pain? Trust and have faith in God's Eternal Word, and be of good courage. When you look up into those dark, rain-soaked skies, observe with awe and wonder the glory of God's creative power, as displayed in the beauty of His Eternal Rainbow.

Your heart will be instantly filled with unspeakable joy, when you reach that spiritual place, where you finally realize, that after every dark period of intense sorrow, sadness, heartache or pain, the soothing sunlight of God's Grace will show up. He'll keep you, protect you, provide warmth, comfort, and cover you in His eternal, abiding love.

The dark, devastating, effects of recent violent storms are temporary, and will last for a brief period of time. Patiently wait, and enjoy the rest that comes from the power of God's Eternal Word, as He commands, the sun to shine after every stormy day. There will never be any kind of storm, in nature or in life that will ever prevent God's everlasting mercy, love and grace from shining in your life. God alone can end all of the negative affects that have come your way, resulting from something that happened on some distant past, stormy, rain-filled day.

God promised, that He'd never again destroy the Earth with water caused by the rain. The Word proclaims peace and rest to the faithful, with a reassuring sign, beautifully placed within the rainbow that commands the *"sun to always shine, after every, stormy, rain-filled day."*

Thomas Paul Monday

Elaine: A Priceless Gift of Enduring Love

The Great I Am, the Creator and Grand Designer of the entire universe, has given us yet another priceless gift displayed through the life of Elaine. She was a visiting, angelic ambassador, temporarily on assignment from a very secret place; secure from all prying eyes. It's carefully hidden somewhere within the vast universe we lovingly call space. This special place is called Heaven, and lay far, far beyond any reach of the five physical senses, that govern this material realm in which we now live. To date, man has been unable through the power of his own intellect and his mechanical brilliance to successfully locate or observe the celestial shores of this wonderful, breathtaking place.

The Divine Word spoke eons ago and creative laws began to produce. Elaine was fashioned with an abundance of patience, elegance and enduring love, but became severely restricted by the physical limitations of illness that eventually befalls all human beings born of mortal clay. Elaine gladly accepted her assignment, and was sent to another minute spot in the universe, on loan to a place called planet Earth. It was just one prayer's breath away from the celestial shores in paradise, that she knew by faith was home. The Creator granted Elaine a temporary visitor's Visa, in this life before the very foundations of creation were even formed, affording her an opportunity to create countless cherished memories with her husband, Chuck, and their daughter, Lauren. Today, we celebrate the precious gift of her life, which appears to all of us, was extremely too short.

Elaine accepted the invitation for a safe passage, from the King of Peace, to reside in His eternal rest, before and during her journey home, over that treacherous highway that all must travel. This is that final journey through a land possessed by the destroyer of all humanity, that old mortal enemy we call "Death." The journey begins when we each, leave behind these old earthly vessels that are made from the potter's pallet, containing lumps of moist clay. On that day, in the mere blink of an eye, we'll begin to fly away leaving behind all sorrow, heartache, suffering and pain. We'll travel faster than the speed of light, until we arrive at our final grand destination, and then wonder in amazement, why we hadn't come any sooner.

Elaine was deeply loved by her husband, her daughter, the extended family, neighbors, co-workers and a host of loving friends. Elaine will certainly be truly missed, but never forgotten. The priceless contents within the treasure chest of Elaine's eternal spirit overflowed continually with natural beauty, both from within and outward. She deeply enriched the lives of everyone that she met. Thoughts and fond memories of countless moments long past, quietly rise to the surface in the form of joy from somewhere deep within the heart, into the stillness of the night sky, like smoke escaping from the confines of a burning candle, Divinely placed on the sacred altar of the soul, as an everlasting, living memorial. A Memorial smoke that continually mixes and mingles together only has one defining purpose, and that is to become reunited with the Creator.

This is not the end, but just another bend in the road, before entering that final stretch toward home. Put your trust and faith in Him and He'll safely see you through from start to finish. Then you'll truly be able to say with the upmost of confidence, like a bird released into the sky from a long confinement in a prison cage, today, I'm going to fly away. I'll see you there.

Thomas Paul Monday

Abstracts of a Thankful Heart

Silence radiates through the quiet stillness of the night, long after the sun has surrendered the last of its strength; thus causing a multitude of dormant thoughts deep down within the storehouse of the soul to boil with restless discontent. Thoughts like volcanic molten lava, erupting in search of some desperate means of escape from the depths of its eternal confinement.

Multiple thoughts erupted into the night sky, like exploding fireworks, scattering deformed bat-like illuminations in every direction, in desperate search of prey. The complexities of the content of my thoughts appear to rise higher and higher, as they become entangled in the fierceness of a sudden wind.

Escape, escape quickly, and use the cloak of the darkness. Escape and ease the pressure on this my weary heart, now void of any form of lasting happiness. The prison cell that once held my troubled soul captive is completely empty.

A Smile Made of Pure Gold, Delma

The pure, natural warmth that comes from the radiance of a beautiful smile always has a positive thawing affect in softening the hard surface of any potential adversary.

In the stillness of the night, while listening to the smooth, soothing sounds of the music slowly oozing from the speakers, I meditated on the attributes that make up those priceless qualities found deep within the treasure chest of the human spirit.

My thoughts of one particular encounter with a young lady named Delma, had a very profound affect on me, leaving a lasting impression that could have only been accomplished by the authentic beauty of a genuine smile.

The captivating affects of such a wonderful smile will ultimately leave any unsuspecting recipient mesmerized and completely blown away.

The sheer charm of that wonderful smile gave only a short peek of the love, and caring character that you inherently possessed. Many of these qualities of your natural beauty had already been discovered by most of your family members, close friends, and co-workers years ago.

Superficial beauty may be only skin deep, but pure eternal beauty, flows quite naturally from an artesian spring: deep from within the sacred altar of the soul. It continues to make lasting impressions to others through the five senses, accented by an infectiously captivating smile.

I was saddened to learn of your passing, but when I remembered the warmth and beauty of that very lovely smile, I felt a quiet peace come over me, as a still voice spoke softly to my heart, saying;

"Don't worry or fret about my passing, for you see, I've completed the task that my Heavenly Father had assigned to me. And so, I've been transferred to my new, eternal celestial home, where the beauty of a smile is still worth its weight in pure gold."

I Want To Be Just Like You, Horn

While quietly laying on my recliner, temporary suspended in time by the dark stillness of the night, with my eyes firmly fixed on the spot that I perceived might lead to the locked door that housed the precious contents of the human spirit.

Sweet, soothing, sounds of music from multiple speakers, cleverly hidden somewhere within the confines of the darkness, quietly begin to invade: slowly overpowering the sentries standing guard in defense of my "inner-sanctuary," a mortal fortress made from dirt and clay.

Multiple explosions create a breach through the wall of the "inner-sanctuary," exposing and eventually extinguishing that eternal flame that had once burned so brightly on the sacred altar of my soul.

Countless thoughts about the extinguished flame, like the smoke that quickly escapes from a recently extinguished flame, and rise suddenly from the sacred altar of the soul into the air only to then disappear.

There are continuous thoughts and fond memories of a hardworking, loving husband and father, who possessed a lot of pride in the upbringing of his all his kids; the three that he voluntary raised or adopted, as well as, the two of his very own.

Although he never actually learned to read or write, my daddy was a big, big success in my eyes, because he had a good woman: my loving mother by his side to encourage, and to assist him in providing for the family.

The love and kindness that my daddy displayed as a man, regarding providing for his family has had a profound affect on my life, by boldly, and continually modeling those basic core values that I now hold so dear as an adult.

Horn, I miss you and I love you. I refuse to let the flame of righteousness become extinguished on the sacred altar of my soul, because daddy, *"I want to be just like you."*

Precious Poetic Moments

If The Heavenly Father Truly Didn't Care, Patricia

There are times when the pain and sorrows of this old world overflow the sacred boundaries of the river that feeds the fertile valley of my soul.

Quite often, one calamity or disaster seemingly appears one right after another, far, far too many for one individual to simply bear silently all alone.

It's during those trying moments, when I find myself, in pain asking the question, "Does the Lord of Glory, the Creator of both the heavens and the Earth truly care?"

There is always an immediate response and my mind is put at ease, with a refreshing comforting thought, whispered in the ear, by the soothing voice of the Holy Spirit, saying,

"My grace is sufficient for you, and it's all you need. Now, I want you to consider the love, mercy and grace that I gave to my servant Job."

The Lord of Glory, who is also called, The Great I AM is no respecter of persons. He cannot lie and He does not change.

God's grace is sufficient for you, and it's all you need.

Why would God, the Father permit His only begotten Son, to be abused, humiliated, and laden with the sins of all humanity? Finally, why would the Heavenly Father allow an only Son to be crucified by being nailed to a cross on a hill called Calvary?

God's Son shed his precious blood, just to redeem you and I, thereby affording us the opportunity to obtain everlasting life.

Thomas Paul Monday

God's grace is sufficient for you, and it's all you need.

Why wouldn't God have given my all, the best I had, with enduring eternal love, mercy, and grace, if He truly didn't care?

Eternal Loving Memory of Coach

Coach was a very precious gift that had the profound affect of change in the lives of everyone he met. Ed was energy-in-motion, a continuous source of encouragement and inspiration.

Coach possessed the ability to motivate a person into activating the richness of joy that comes from a, "Can Do Spirit" that once lay dormant, hidden in fertile ground, somewhere within the sacred valley of the soul.

Coach, In Loving Memory Always

Thomas Paul Monday

Thank You Daryl for The Beautiful Landscape Design of My Home: It's a Job Well Done

As I sit on my front porch early in the morning, enjoying a cup of coffee, I'm just beginning to see the first rays of the sun, as it starts to crest the shadowy, dark mountains in the East. I'm overwhelmed with thoughts of awe and wonder of the natural, creative design that went into the landscape construction of my yard.

The rays of fresh warm sunlight have now created a brightly-colored rainbow that reflects so elegantly off the water from the sprinklers just turned on to water the lawn.

As I feel and smell the freshness of the early morning breeze going across my face, there appears to be a quiet still voice that whispers, "Daryl, it's a job well done."

Thoughts and fond memories far, far too great to even consider counting rise up within my spirit like smoke seeking escape from the confines of a consuming fire now starting to burn on the sacred altar of my soul.

It doesn't seem like it was all that long ago, when I was working out in the yard. Daryl just happened to have been driving by and stopped to introduce himself as the creative designer of the landscape for my home.

We talked for over an hour about design ideas, discussing various kinds of plants. Each sharing a common enjoyment that comes from constructing a variety of picturesque, creative landscape designs.

Precious Poetic Moments

There is a Biblical scripture that says, "From the abundance of the heart, the mouth speaks," and that also has to be true about Daryl. His heart overflows with a love for life and he lived it to the fullest. He was a blessing to all that knew him. Daryl cared about others and was willing to share what he had learned from some of the pitfalls in life.

When I've taken that last sip of coffee and head back in the house, I look back over my right shoulder with a smile and say.

"Thank You Daryl For The Beautiful Landscape Design Of My Home. It's a Job Well Done"

Thomas Paul Monday

A Final Thought

I'm thankful to God, just to be here. I'm eternally grateful for His strength and wisdom to allow me to complete this degree. I'd like to acknowledge, the presence of the entire Fielding Staff seated on the podium, and I'd also like to thank my wife, Cortess, and my family for all of their help and support over these past two years.

Two years ago, through the encouragement of a co-worker and a very good friend, (Roger), I was introduced to Fielding Graduate University. My Capstone Project was on using the Constructivist Teaching Approach in the classroom to increase self-esteem of incarcerated youth.

I work with incarcerated youth along with Roger Garcia. Many of these young people come to our facility badly broken, both physically and spiritually. Many of these young men also come from dysfunctional homes, and some have been abused. The majority of these young men are incarcerated because of drug abuse, gang activity and a wide range of acts of violence toward others. They are very hostile and very angry. They range in age from 11 to 19. They read somewhere at the first and second grade levels, and have been repeatedly told they have no worth or social value.

Through my evaluation, I have discovered that if you can improve the self-esteem of these young people and belief in theirselves, then just about anything is possible. I have personally witnessed phenomenal academic change and growth in many of these young men, (both academic and mental growth from self-insight).

It didn't take very long to notice that there was something exceptionally different about Fielding Graduate University's philosophy and commitment to education that made it stand out from all of the rest of the traditional schools of higher education.

I quickly formed a professional partnership with Fielding Graduate University and thus began the journey or quest for a Masters of Arts Degree in Collaborative Educational Leadership (MACEL). I had no idea at the time; just how much Fielding Graduate University and the MACEL program would impact my life's professional career as an educator. I have formed a professional friendship through Fielding Graduate University and the Antelope Valley MACEL Community that will last a lifetime.

Our two facilitators (Sharon and Monique) did an outstanding job in allowing our community to grow and develop into its own. Through the various reading assignments, films, discussions and group collaborations, I was introduced to the true concept of community. We learned about the Constructivism Method of Instruction, its impact on students and how it's different from other standard methods of academic instruction.

In closing, I am grateful to have been a part of Fielding Graduate University and the MACEL program. This experience has afforded me the opportunity to re-energize my spirit and renew my professional commitment to become a better educator.

Thomas Paul Monday

Glory Land Bound, Frankie

I'm an alien visitor, simply passing through, stopping for a brief, but very specific period of time. I find myself stranded in a strange land that's really not my home. I'm just on temporary loan, being permitted to spend some memorable moments with relatives, loved ones, family and very precious friends, all of who I will truly miss.

The very day I came into this world, by way of a human birth, I was also automatically given an appointment that would one-day end in physical death, because of Adam's fall from grace through his disobedience, rebellion and sin.

It's the sincere desire of each visitor, temporarily stranded within the restricted confines of these mortal suits, to one day end their earthly stay, and to go home to live with the Father in His Majestic Celestial Home.

Every person born must pay the same price through death, but only the righteous, those who have accepted Jesus Christ, and what He did on the cross at Calvary, through His redeeming blood, will be allowed to pass from death to eternal life.

Christ's victory on Calvary, when He openly defeated the devil, by taking from him, the keys of death, hell and the grave, gave every believer the right to live throughout eternity with the Father in Paradise.

There are vast multitudes of travelers that occupy the broad road that lead to destruction, but only a very few travelers will find and occupy the narrow path that leads to true everlasting rest.

Everyone has a specifically appointed moment in time, when we all will pull off these old corrupted bodies of mortal earthen clay, through the process called death. However, as believers, we have as assurance Jesus' victory over death. We will leave these old bodies of earthly clay behind, and will awake in the presence of the Lord, with new glorified celestial bodies.

Please don't worry or fret regarding my change in residence. I am happy, and resting in the Lord. I have finished the race that was set before me, while I possessed that old earthly house of mortal clay, and now I claim as my permanent home of residence, a much grander place. I now reside with the King of Kings, with unspeakable peace, joy, and beauty, in a place divinely called, "The Glory Land."

Thomas Paul Monday

Got Time for a Dime

If I could turn back the hands of time, I wouldn't waste any time, fussing or cursing or drinking wine. You see, I'd be studying and learning, trying to get the most time for my dimes.

Someone once told me that fine is fine, but I'd better make the most of the commodity called time, because it doesn't wait for anyone. Yeah, I could have sworn that I was right and the person was wrong. But friend, here I am at 33, (that's three score and three), with years of time completely gone).

I'm told that success is determined by a very simple formula, hard work plus study,

Multiplied by time. Might this be why I can't keep a dime?

Maybe, if I had been more independent and productive with my time, I wouldn't,

Have a need for things that can be purchased with so many dimes of time.

Regrets

They say life is what you make it. Yours might be a life filled with many regrets. Have you ever considered that your worst enemy was someone whom, you at one time thought was your best friend?

This brings too much pain to be love. Every day, it's the same old routine. I relive soulful moments of painful regrets. There's nothing but heartache and pain. I live with no way out or any way to escape. I'm tired of this. Without tears and regrets, I realize that I've created my own torment.

Thomas Paul Monday

Honey in High Heels

What is as sweet as sugar, and prettier than a dozen fresh, cut roses? What is tastier than a chilled glass of fine, vintage wine, and lovelier than a summer Sunset, on the beach?

Naturally, there can be only one conclusive answer, the sight of pure honey walking in high heels.

Special Person

On numerous occasions, I've been told by many different people, that an,

Angel is perhaps the prettiest of all created beings. I'm also told that these,

Lovely entities, reside somewhere in the spirit realm, in a wonderful place called Heaven.

Whether this is fact or fiction, no one actually knows, so I'll just let you decide,

For yourself whether or not angels are a reality.

The plain fact of the matter, however, that these exquisitely gorgeous beings possess only a fraction of the beauty and splendor that you share daily with so many.

Now, looking at you, I understand more clearly just why angels are there.

Thomas Paul Monday

The Radiance of Beauty

The elegance and radiance of your beauty, which is enhanced by the sweetness of,

Your name, can truly only serve one meaningful purpose and that is, to magnify the,

Glory, from the wealth of pure natural honey, contained within the depth less well of your soul.

Alone

I can tell that look in your eye, and by the bed spread on the bed, that it must be 10:25.

Darkness gives away to the light, fear gives way to joy, death gives way to life, and,

Loneliness gives way to companionship.

I'm a king on the way home, yet, deep within; I know that once more, I'll soon be,

Dethroned, then, darkness and once again reclaim my home.

The time 10:25 makes me strong and gives me hope, that just this once, just maybe, I'll remain the king of my home.

As 10:25, approach, you don your mask, with its displayed act of kindness, from the Long dead past.

The true purpose, which apparently, only I can see, is to give to others that which was openly stolen from me.

When the clock strikes 10:25, it, seems to sets me free, to live life as it was meant to be, but, because of an abundance of lies all mingled together with false hope, I remain a slave to a myth, believing to this very second, and that perhaps you do really love me.

The joyous music of 10:25, has come and gone, proving once more that, I will never be a king in this home.

Thomas Paul Monday

Diamonds, Roses and a Cube of Sugar from the Entire Challenger School Staff

Judith, what do you have in common, with the three items in the title above?

Judith, you are a hard worker, a dedicated co-worker and a friend. You're very knowledgeable and are always willing to help. You firmly believe that things should be done the right way. Truly a person like you, in today's' world is a precious commodity, pretty much like a rare and priceless diamond.

The beauty of life is being able to affect change in the lives of others. Beauty is all around us, if only we take a moment or two to look for it, or its source. The beauty that you possess, I truly believe comes from the very essence of the soul and is just as natural as the loveliness of a very beautiful rose.

Patience, I'm told is a virtue. If this is true, then patience must also be associated with sweetness. You have a very unique way of dealing with problems and difficulty. I've observed you on numerous occasions masterfully use the sweetness of patience. You always know just how much sweetness to use, one sugar cube or sometimes two.

Judith, best of luck in your new position. We also want you to know that we've appreciated everything that you've done over the years, to help keep a healthy working relationship between probation and the school.

If It Were Possible the Two of US

If it were possible the two of us would command the bright, warm rays of the sun to blot out all of the darkness and sadness that this tragic death has produced.

If it were possible, the two of us, would turn all of your hurt and pain into smoke; allowing it to escape forever into the dark, stillness of the night, rather than being forever confined in the sacred treasure of the soul.

If it were possible the two of us, would give you the wings of an eagle so you might soar far above all of the negative thoughts and images of the past.

And yes, if it were possible, we would ensure that you would also possess the eyes the eagle, so that you could look instinctively into the eyes of Jesus for His direction and guidance. He's the one who holds the keys to life and death. It is Jesus and Him alone, who can boldly proclaim, I'm the Alpha and the Omega.

If it were possible, the two of us would open the storehouse of our hearts and present you with an overflowing abundance of love during this time of loss.

Tricia, we love you. Our thoughts and prayers are with you, always.

Sincerely,

The Two of US.

Thomas Paul Monday

Oh, Bless the Lord; My Debt Was Paid In Full, Praise His Holy Name, Ricky

Oh, bless the Lord, oh, my soul. Oh, bless the Lord, oh, my soul. Oh, bless the Lord, forever more, giving all honor, eternal praise, and worship, to the Lord of all. He's the Creator of everything; both in the heavens, on the earth. Oh, bless the Lord, oh, my soul. Oh, praise the Lord, forever more.

Oh, bless the Lord, oh, bless the Lord, oh my soul. Oh, bless the Lord, oh bless the Lord, oh my soul. Oh, bless His holy Name forever more, and He's powerful and mighty. He's the Great I AM; He's a mighty conqueror and He's King of Kings. Oh, praise the Lord, oh my soul, oh praise the Lord, forever more.

Oh, bless the Lord, Oh, bless the Lord, oh, my soul. praise His mighty and holy name. Oh, bless the Lord, a Name that above every other Name, Oh, come on, why can't you give Him honor, praise and respect, because there's awesome power in His Name. Oh, bless the Lord, oh bless the Lord, oh my soul. Oh, praise the Lord, all day long and even forever more.

Oh, bless the Lord, oh, bless the Lord, oh my soul forever more, Creator of everything, in the heavens, on the earth, and everything in between. Oh, bless the Lord oh my soul forever more. Oh, bless the Lord, oh my soul forever more. Oh, bless the Lord, praising the Lord's Name. Oh my soul forever and forever.

Oh, bless the Lord, oh bless the Lord. Oh, bless the Lord, oh my soul. Heavenly Father, please accept my burnt offering of praise, thanksgiving, admiration and respect, as they rise like incense from a sacrifice strapped to the sacred altar of the soul, toward Heaven's Celestial, Eternal Shores. Oh, bless the Lord. Oh, bless the Lord, with my heart, body, spirit and soul. Oh, bless the Lord, oh my soul, allowing praises to His Holy Name to flow continually from my mouth.

Oh, bless the Lord. Oh, bless the Lord. Oh, bless the Lord, oh my soul with every ounce of strength that's contained within my being. To praise His Name, for what He did for you and I on the cross, high on top of a lonely hill called Calvary. Oh, bless the Lord. Oh, bless the Lord. Oh, bless the Lord. Oh, my soul sing praise with joy and honor just to mention His precious Name. Oh, bless the Lord. Oh, bless the Lord. Oh, give praise to the Lord of glory and King of Kings. Oh, bless the Lord, oh, my soul.

Oh, bless the Lord. Oh, bless the Lord. Oh, bless the Lord, oh my soul, thanking God always for purchasing my debt, paying it in full. Thus setting me free of all shame, pain, sickness and guilt. He did it for all humanity, through the washing, and regeneration power of His redemptive blood. If you're truly grateful and not ashamed, say the following out loud, "Oh, bless the Lord, our Eternal Father, and the King has purchased all of our sins as if they were His Own, and Has Paid Them off in Full, Oh Praise His Holy Name."

Thomas Paul Monday

Change Might Be a Necessity, But Here's My Final Thought

Quietly reflecting on a thought that was discussed at the start of the group or upon one of the many inspiring quotations, which seemed to bridge the abyss of self-doubt and depression, through the richness of hope.

Thoughts of gratitude rises swiftly, and quietly, into the darkness of the night sky, like smoke seeking escape from the confines of a fire that rages out-of-control somewhere on the defiled wounded altar of my soul.

Collectively, reflections and thoughts being birthed, are too numerous to jot down on this single sheet of paper, regarding all the ways in which you have been able to positively affect change in the lives of so many.

You've skillfully guided, encouraged and listened objectively to all who chose to participate. I've observed how you've professionally educated your group attendees, stuck in the pain of their own individual temptations and trials. I've seen how you've effectively used such affective techniques, like gentle kinds words of encouragement, mixed with insight and hope, especially when they seek answers to the question "why."

In the evolution of professional friendships, there is never such a thing as "goodbye."

We, the members of your various groups, "thank you," for all of your help, guidance, and wish you the very best that the future holds.

The Eternal Twins,
They Call Henry and Ed

How does one define the true meaning of what a friendship should be or how much time needs to pass, before one can say with any certainty and confidence that a friendship actually exists?

Over the past thirteen years, I've been blessed to have had the opportunity to observe first-hand, the love and respect for one another that developed over a period of years, between two particularly very special individuals, my co-workers **Henry and Ed.**

The friendship that has developed between the two of them and their,

Immediate families have weathered the test of time, both through the good time, as well as, through the rough times.

While reflecting on some of the key ingredients that seem to have solidified their friendship over the past twenty-five (25) years, my thoughts and memories quickly began to rise into the night sky of my spirit, like smoke seeking escape from the confines of a raging fire, now burning out-of-control on the sacred altar of my soul.

With a smile, I remembered a phrase that Henry once said, that I guess somewhat identifies and sums up the foundational truth on which their long-standing friendship is firmly-based.

Henry once said, "I can lie to you and you might even lie to me, but we aren't going to lie to each other."

A true friend, oftentimes, is closer to you than a natural blood brother, and will tell you what you may or may not really want to hear, but yet he still has your back, through thick and thin.

How can one care about others, if he doesn't first love, respect and care about himself?

There is no greater demonstration of love, than for a person to be willing to lay down his own life, in order to save the life of a friend.

The Eternal friends, the twins, Henry and Ed.

A Quiet, Soft-Spoken, Gentle Giant, Bill

Today we mourn the passing of a truly wonderful, caring mentor, friend and co-worker. He was a soft-spoken man, but a giant amongst his family, community, church, associates and countless, countless, friends.

Sitting quietly within the confines of my easy chair, my thoughts of him go back in time, to that day when we were first introduced. I became immediately impressed with his quiet demeanor, professionalism, knowledge, and desire to see people improve socially and economically.

Bill was a wonderful husband, married to the same woman for over 50 years. He was a strong pillar within his church and community, always giving the Lord credit for any success that he may have obtained.

He was a quiet man, but his giant strides, left a lasting impression with all. As I reflect back over the years, that I have known him, I can see the many treasures and legacies that dot the landscape: announcing to all that with the help of the Lord, Bill has truly passed through.

The Lord had given him, his assignment, which he gladly accepted wholeheartedly. His task plain and simple was to reach the world for Jesus Christ, while teaching others to achieve success through education.

The Lord of Glory recently announced that Bill's earthly assignment had been completed, and that he would be reassigned to another home of residence, somewhere along the eternal, celestial shores, where the streets were made of pure diamonds and gold.

Thomas Paul Monday

He would have to leave behind his old worn, tired, earthly vessel made from mortal clay, in exchange for one that represented his new assignment in paradise, where once again he'd be required to sing praises to the King, and the Lord of Glory, as he walked with a newfound purpose among new giants.

A Precious Gift, He Gave To Me

I can still vividly remember with awe, as a young child one Sunday, I guess I couldn't have been any younger than 3 or 4, when several folks in our small church congregation, during the morning service gave their life to Christ and were baptized.

The preacher said that they were now new creatures in Christ and were part of the family of the Almighty King of Glory. It was right then, that I firmly made up my mind that I also wanted to become a member of this happy and loving eternal family.

Knowing the desires of a precious pure little heart, my Heavenly Father first sent the Holy Spirit to teach me about the eternal love story concerning His Son, Jesus' and just how much that He truly cared about me. I opened the door of my heart to Jesus and He came right in, immediately began the removal, by faith all evidence of my past sins.

I received baptism of The Holy Spirit, through the Love of my parents, Sunday school teachers, relatives and a host of forgotten others. I meditated on His holy Word. I was also taught all about God's everlasting and immeasurable love. I learned about His mercy, and the eternal grace that Jesus had been holding in reserve just for me, a divine plan that He had made before the very foundations of the world was ever laid.

There is something that I feel must be said, about being able to receive, such a priceless gift with the pure expectant faith and innocence of a precious little child. Truly if you believe and doubt not in your heart, you will receive whatever you've been asking and praying for.

Thomas Paul Monday

Dear Heavenly Father, when this life's work that you have assigned is done, allow me to just walk around in glory shouting out praise, alone with the rest of the Heavenly host, who also lift up praise, thanksgiving and worship, "Holy, Holy, Holy is Your Great Name, with honor and thanksgiving forever Now, Always and Forever Worthy to Be Eternally Praised."

Remembering forever, the priceless Gift of Jesus the precious blood of Jesus, Who was born, taught us the Love of God, His Father, who was rejected by the Jews and humanity. The Divine Gift that permitted Himself to suffer on a cross, while bearing the sins of all mankind, thereby affording humanity the opportunity, mercy and salvation through faith in the saving grace of the redemptive blood Christ.

The only Gift that has been given a name above all other names, in both heaven and Earth that can save a lost soul from permanent eternal damnation. I'm eternally grateful, for the precious blood of Jesus, and the sacrifice of what Christ had to endure by being nailed to a cross. *Jesus is truly, "A Very Precious Gift to Me."*

My Mother Joann

A Source of Unconditional Enduring Love

Mom, loving thoughts and memories of you rise swiftly into the night sky, seeking escape from the confines of a sad, bitter fire, now raging out-of-control, centered somewhere on the wounded altar of my abandoned soul.

Memories of laughter, that I thought long ago, I had forgotten, now spring up within my spirit as a source of help, and strength during this time of loss.

The reason why you had to leave your earthly home, so soon will remain another unsolved mystery during this brief period of travel in space and time, called "life."

There are words of hope and comfort that have stood the test of time.

There's a time, a reason and a season for everything. Although we know we don't fully understand, we still ask the question, "Why?" There's a time to laugh and a time to cry. There's a time to work, and when you've labored long enough, there's even a time to rest.

The memorializing of precious memories will bridge the dark abyss of any sudden, tragic loss. It will also renew the soul with a highly-cherished, commodity: one in which we so affectionately call, "a mother's endearing unconditional love."

Memories and thoughts of you, continually radiate upwards and out, celebrating the love you gave to so many and all of the lives that you touch in such a brief period in time.

There is resurrecting power, and life giving strength in the blood!

Thomas Paul Monday

Surrounded with endless love from the very beginning of time eternal, you'll arise transformed, as you eagerly await that rebirth into the brilliance of a brand new day, filled with the warmth, peace and beauty that only the God of the universe can provide through belief in His Son.

A Temporary Loan from Heaven, Edna

I'm reminded daily of just how brief this period of mortal existence can truly be. I read in the scriptures that life on Earth is like a breeze, which awakens early in the morning totally unannounced, traveling across the surface of the ground unrestrained, fulfilling its divine purpose. Once its job is done, it is equally as quiet, as it fades away, leaving few clues, if any, as to where it's gone.

Lying quietly on my bed in the dark stillness of the night, my mind began to wonder, as my thoughts roamed, concerning the great mysteries of the universe or a few simple little things that very has struck.

It is on those rare occasions that many people feel the most vulnerable, because it leaves them hurt, sad, or mad with a kind of eerie, creepy feeling that comes from being totally abandoned and left all alone.

Thoughts too numerous to even count, started rising quickly up into the sky, like hot, steamy vapors, seeking escape from open, containers of water, left abandoned on the fiery asphalt of a deserted freeway leading to the sacred altar of my soul,

My thoughts soon turned to all of my friends, and loved ones who've been born or who have recently transitioned from life to death and now rest, patiently awaiting, for what many seniors lovingly call "That Great Getting Up Day."

Lastly I had to consider, the very air that I breathe each second of the day. This too, has a divine purpose and is a precious gift from the Creator above, The Great I AM.

Thomas Paul Monday

This World is not my home; I'm on a temporary assignment.

Don't worry, or fret about those of us who sleep, you see, we have fulfilled our life assignments and have returned home, because we were only "*A Temporary Loan from Heaven.*"

Something That Mama Once Said

In the stillness of the night, I sometimes find myself reflecting back in time, concerning many of my life trials and a host of very special events.

Quite often, I relive numerous very special loving events as a child with those day-to-day interactions with one, if not both of my parents.

When my dad died on July 4, 1969, my mother, found herself alone. Since she married my father, but decided that she had her stuff and enjoyed being independent, so she decided to continue to live in her home of over 50-plus years.

Although she lived alone, all of my brothers and isters, except me and an older sister, still lived within the same city, where my mother also lived and we all had grown up.

Since I lived fifty-seven (57) miles away, I would try to drive down, to check on her every other week or so, but I'd always call her every Sunday.

When I drove down, I'd always stop by McDonald's, to get my mother a deluxe pancake breakfast meal, and a small cup of hot coffee.

Then we'd just sit and talk.

Quite often during our talk, I would ask the question, or in one-way or another the question would invariably come up, "Mama, don't you get lonely, and how can you stay here all by yourself?"

She would always give me a big smile and then give the same answer, saying, "Son, I don't get lonely, and I'm never alone, because it's been me and Jesus, since I was a little girl."

Thomas Paul Monday

Tears

Countless tears of sadness flow forcefully down the sides of my cheeks, like collective raindrops, forming ribbons of running water that quickly falls from a steeply pitched roof, right in the midst of a cold winter rain.

Crying together, holding and kissing one another,

I still reminiscence about how we first met, and verbalizing just what we really mean to each other.

All of my thoughts and memories, are too numerous to even count.

There are mountains of joy, heartache, sadness and even pain, was it really necessary, or was it inadvertently, just another part of life's treacherous game?

In retrospect, all of my tears, were needed to collectively form a stream and then a raging river, in order to be united as one, that it might be forcibly pushed by the majestic power of gravity downhill, and away from my torn, wounded and broken soul.

Eventually, in due time and in its own season, I forgave and let go.

My Creator, is faithful, and He's always on time, initiating divine healing, allowing me to get stronger, with each new passing day, putting ever increasing amounts of space and time, between me, you, and the past.

That Fall From Grace

Shaken and awaken, slowly rising from a prison of lifeless sleep, somewhere deep within the confines of that bottomless pit, seeking to reclaim the freedom and the power that he thought somewhere in the distant past, once was his.

The Deceiver, now certified and commissioned, with a legal license in hand unites the forces of darkness, to seek out and attack the light, with strict instructions to seduce and to recruit, as they go forth throughout the land, seeking ...

Converts, are never told of the soon impending date with death, destruction, and everlasting damnation. This being the final destination and just reward, for all of those who have fallen. Those who for one reason or another in life refused to bend a knee to call on His name and seek His unconditional forgiveness in return for His loving eternal mercy.

According to the Word, the divine architect of the universe and Creator of everything therein, who is also sometimes called, The Bread of Life" "The Great I AM, "The Alpha and the Omega," just to name a few of His divine names, He is well able.

My God, already knew, and had a plan in place, which He had designed and predestined from the very foundations of the world, culminating with everlasting rest and peace with Him, in our new heavenly home.

Thomas Paul Monday

Tricia If It Were Possible, the Two of Us, *In Memory of Eldrew*

If it were possible, the two of us would command the bright, warm rays of the sun to blot out all of the sadness and darkness that this tragic event has produced.

If it were possible, the two of us, would turn your hurt and pain into smoke.

If it were possible, the two of us, would command the smoke from your hurt and pain to rise into the stillness of the night sky and silently disappear, forever into eternity.

And if it were possible, the two of us would give you the wings of an eagle so that you might soar far above all of the negative thoughts and images of the past.

And yes it were possible, we would insure that you would also possess eyes of the eagle so that you could look instinctively into the eyes of the Son for direction and guidance.

The one who holds the keys to life and death, who boldly proclaims that he is the Alpha and the Omega.

If it were possible, the two of us would open the treasure chests our souls, and present you with eternal gifts of friendships and love, during this time of loss.

Tricia, we love you. Our thoughts and prayers are with you always.

Sincerely
The Two of Us

Precious Poetic Moments

A Co-Worker, Neighbor, Mentor and a Friend

What do you say to someone who has dedicated an entire life to the quest of knowledge and the education of others?

Sometimes the seeds of education cast on the soil of the soul, often take time to mature and evolve into what it's destined to become.

Periodically, we pause to honor specific moments of commitment and valor as the hands of time move inconspicuously along the halls of eternity.

Today is one such event, as we pause to celebrate and acknowledge the culmination of the long and distinguished career of Charlie Pipers.

We will always remember your leadership, professionalism and reflective thoughts as you've attempted to dispel the darkness and ignorance within the human heart, through the sunshine of enlightenment.

Charlie, you are not vanishing just transitioning into a new phase of life, and to another level of things you have always enjoyed doing.

I believe from the treasure chest of your soul, your love for humanity will continue to grow, even in this new and exciting adventure.

Charlie, never cease to be a fisherman for humanity, as you journey to these exciting new ports.

We the entire Challenger staff, love you and wish you the very best.

Thomas Paul Monday

The Day Mother Became an Angel

It has been said that a woman's name is, a reflection of only a small portion of the many beautiful gifts that are stored deep within the treasure chest of her soul. If in fact, this is the case, then some treasures chests must be overflowing with an abundance of these precious gifts, when compared to others.

The other day, while at home relaxing, I had the very special privilege and opportunity, to talk on the telephone with a very beautiful lady, my mother, Mrs. Priscilla.

This beautiful lady, is now 86 (eight score and six years young) four score and six years young, and through the Grace of God, is still going strong. She has been in the same house for over fifty years (50 years in the same house?) She's still able to take care of herself, do house own house work, and on occasion perform a little yard work out side. Yes, it was during and after our conversation that I became keenly aware of the knowledge and wisdom that this sweet lady has come to possess, over the many years of walking around on this Earth.

She has developed an unshakeable, rock-like faith and trust in the daily study of her Heavenly Father's Word. Like a true mother, one that really cares, she always reminds all of her children to: pray, study God's Word, and to put their faith and trust in the Word of God to save our soul in a dying day.

I've been told on numerous occasions, by many different people, that there are angels, walking amongst those of us that makeup, what we call the family of humanity. And, that angels, perhaps, are the prettiest of all the created beings. It's been said, that these elegant beings possess the ability to turn sadness into joy, with just the twinkle in their eyes, or with something as simple as a kind word, ensued by the warmth and beauty of a very pretty smile.

Precious Poetic Moments

I decided to do a little research, and look up the name Priscilla, just to see what it meant. I discovered that Priscilla is from a Latin word that means, "from ancient times." The richness of this woman's, dedication to her God and family, only added to the glory that she already possessed.

I am deeply intrigued with the life of this woman: her contributions and the numerous talents that she possessed. I truly admired her faith and courage, during the good times, as well as, during the sad. She is the rock, that each of us learned to hold on to, during the storm, when the sea of life turned rough and violent.

Mama, is the one, when each of us is far away, we try to get back to, because wherever mama is, that's the place we call "home."

She's a strong beautiful, Black Woman, a proud mother, and a role model for all of her children. Never once, has she wavered in her love and devotion toward any of them.

She was faithful with what little she had, and therefore God has blessed her greatly in an abundance of years and wisdom.

She possessed and knew how, to daily utilize the wisdom of God, toward the benefits of those around her.

She recognized the true source of her strength, and had wisdom enough, to give God the glory, thanks, and the credit.

She offered her advice to any of us that are willing to take note and hear.

Many, many times we are blessed after her counsel. I believe because she has God's ear.

Thomas Paul Monday

Though I Walk Through the Valley of the Giants (Who Am I)

I am a legend, within my own mind, the master of my universe and the Creator of my own fate

Everything in my world has to evolve around me: standing barely four feet, 3 inches in my shiny black platform shoes.

I strut the walk and talk the talk.

My position and the authority it provides, makes me virtually untouchable just like those real-life tough guys.

Some of my peers call me hateful, arrogant and cruel.

It really does give me great pleasure to see other suffer heartache, financial loss and endure emotional pain, because of something that I may have said or did.

One of my favorite saying is, "Who are people going to believe you or me?"

I manipulate, lie, and cheat to get what I want.

Now I'm permanently stuck in this valley called payback, with no visible way out.

I've come to realize that whatever goes up must also come down.

What goes in must come also come out, and that the reign of justice falls on everyone.

The tables will always turn, even for a small, desperate, cruel, man, with shiny black platform shoes.

I'm just another mortal man, who actually believed, that through my own natural ability, power and strength I could have become another living legend; even if within my own mind, as I try to walk through the valley of the giants.

Thomas Paul Monday

A Smile for Jessie

I remember, back in the day when we were all just family. Doing the thing that real families do, fighting, arguing, laughing, and caring about one another. When I think about how things used to be from just being a little kid, I truly believed that we were all somehow very special. Then, we grew up and went our own separate ways. We eventually grow old and die. Wow! I really miss you, but in just remembering, the thought always produces a very special, loving, smile for Jessie.

Pure Beauty in Flight

While peering into the stillness of the night sky, at stars, far, far too many, to even to gauge. My thoughts of you rise silently up into the night air, lingering there for only a brief moment, only to vanish forever, into the eternal abyss of the soul.

Smiling briefly, while I reminiscence about, my yesterday, today and together, all our countless tomorrows, I'm reminded of the glory and elegance of an Eagle soaring high in the sky, a portrait of sheer grace and beauty suspended permanently within that brief ripple in the universe we call, "time."

Absolute beauty and pure perfection, remains keenly aware, watching with confidence, the events evolving below, on the fertile ground within the soul. The beauty of the Eagle, allows itself to be carried unconsciously by the swift and ever-changing currents of space and time, and yet like you still remain unchanged.

Thomas Paul Monday

A Rose for All Times

Destiny or chance presents itself to opportunity only once and very, very rarely twice. Today, I was fortunate enough to have witnessed a very special event. One of those very rare moments, in which chance, opportunity and timing all converged at the very same point. Many of us routinely refer to this brief abstract point, located somewhere on the time line of infinity, as "Life."

The eternal beauty of a rose, the lasting taste of pure honey, or the peace and serenity, that comes from watching the beginning and the ending of another day. It was perfect timing that I by chance, meet a very delightful young lady named Demetree. Rarely does one have the opportunity, to watch and fully appreciate the actual affect that other people so often have on us, as we are continually exposed to their warmth and beauty.

This young lady is truly a very rare and precious kind of rose. Watch patiently, and you'll observe the warm rays of love continually radiating out to others. Beauty carefully, and quietly from the eternal depths, that resides only in the treasure chest of the soul like the sweet fragrance of perfume floating upwards, toward the surface, only to exit suddenly through the creation of a lovely smile.

The human spirit is essentially held captivated by the essence of that very special sparkle, that's always present each time one looks into your eyes. The lasting effect of a lovely rose is truly eternal and will always be remembered.

Evelyn – All Is Well – My Big Sister

When I first received the tragic news regarding the passing of my best friend and big sister, my thoughts throughout the day, have periodically gone back in time. I so clearly hear within the very depths of my spirit the beautiful melody from the soothing words of the song sang by **Barbara Streisand,** entitled "**The Way We Were**".

Evelyn, as countless precious thoughts, memories and beautiful moments with you continually flow within the depth of my spirit I'm reminded of all of the joyful fun times we had and have shared with each other. It seems as if these fun filled moments took place only recently, perhaps as early as just this morning, during the glorious introduction of the hope, mercy and blessing that can only come experiencing the resurrection power found in the start of another new day.

I so vividly recall the weekly phone conversations that we have had between each other over the years. I remember the enormous pride that I had in you whenever I would refer to you "**my big sister.** The song that the late **Michael Jackson sang,** called "**Gone Too Soon**", only partly describes the true sense of my loss and the disbelief that I feel.

Countless loving thoughts, prayers and fond memories continue to rise silently into the night sky only to vanish like sacred smoke radiating from the, fragrance of incense. These sweet fragrances represen*t* my thoughts, precious memories and moments of you, which flow unhindered, filling the stratosphere of my spirit, securely located just within sight of that eternal treasure chest called the Soul.

Evelyn, although I missed you dearly, I'm comforted in just knowing that you are now resting, in the loving arms of the Savior, our Lord and King, free of all suffering, troubles, heartache and pain. I'm also reminded of the beautiful song, sang by the late **Whitney Huston,** entitled "**As I Look To You**".

It's kind of a mind blowing thought to wondering with awe, just what it is going to be like when you see you Daughter Kim, and others love ones, again. This time the joyful celebrations will last forever. What a glorious thought of you just standing in the presence singing songs of praises to our Heavenly Father, whom we both proudly profess to be also our Lord and King.

It's been said that a day to the Lord is like a thousand years and that when He returns for the rest of His saints; it will be as quick as a blink or the twinkle of an eye. Evelyn, my beloved Big Sister, I am also further comforted by knowing, that you've made Jesus your Lord and Savior. Jesus Christ has defeated Death, Hell, and the Grave forever. Oh praise the Lord that Jesus paid the price and gave the ultimate sacrifice for the redemption of his precious saints.

My Big Sister, I am comforted by the powerful authority that resides within the creative Words of the King, when **He says that "My sheep are not lost, neither can anyone remove them from the palms of His hands."** Evelyn, my loving big sister, take your rest. We'll meet again since you and I both are positioned securely in tender loving arms of Christ Jesus and that His Word will never return void.

I find peace, joy and comfort in knowing according to the WORD, that with my **Big Sister, Evelyn, All Is Well!!**

About the Author

Thomas Paul Monday, was born, January 27, 1949, in small town located in the South Eastern part of California. He served in the Marine Corps, the Army National Guard and Air Force Reserves.

He earned an A.A., B.A., Master's Degree and two Teaching Credentials. Mr. Monday worked as an educator for more than 31 years.

He enjoys traveling, music, and writing. Mr. Monday currently resides in Southern California.

www.ingramcontent.com/pod-product-compliance
Lightning Source LLC
Chambersburg PA
CBHW071704040426
42446CB00011B/1904